*M*anual *L*abor,
*M*aximal *L*ove

susan r horton

Cover photograph, "Susan Sanding," is reproduced
courtesy of photographer R. Kevin Ryan

Back cover photograph courtesy of Dr. Robert Loynd and
Jenni Walz Loynd

Design and computer assistance by Scott Reyburn at
MacAuthorityofcc@me.com

Credit for material cited in epigrams and poems can be found
in "Credit Where Credit's Due," pgs. 114-120.

ISBN 978069296896-3

1. Poetry—2. Memoir

Published in collaboration with CreateSpace, and available
from Amazon.com, Barnes and Noble, and ALibris

Correspondence to:
Susan R. Horton
P.O. Box 187
West Harwich, MA. 02671
susan.horton1@verizon.net

DEDICATION

To feasts on the beach, picnics in parks, baseball and football games, poetry, music, nightly suppers, and to the four who over forty years ago shared these things, their teens, and their father, with me.

The thing as a whole, its quality
as a whole, is what is interesting.

Artist Donald Judd, in
"Specific Objects," (1964)

CONTENTS

I

Every highway leads you prodigal back home,
to the ordinary sidewalks you were born to roam.

From "Ordinary Town," written
by Dave Carter, sung by Tracy
Grammer on their 2001 CD,
"Drum Hat Buddha."

✍ PASSIONS AND PIGEONS

The house is three-quarters of a century old.
Past time to check that its studs haven't turned punky;
that the rafters holding up its roof aren't rotted,
their hangers rusted and unreliable.

A simple bit of fortifying the old
in the house of memory won't suffice.
You're its docent and its curator now.

With a structure this old, it's important
to make sure any joins between the old wood
and the new show; that the old paint and the new
bleed into one another, while leaving
just a trace of the place where they join.
      A tricky job.

Many times a day, the boy living across the
B & O tracks went into and out of the cages
he'd cobbled together at his yard's edge,
just across the tracks from my own.
He was tending the pigeons he loved.
From the swing hung from a branch
of an old buckeye, I watched his tending.

When he died of psittacosis at twelve,
what lessons were absorbed?
Was it pigeons, or passions,
that were dangerous?

Or was it that diligence and passion
brought pleasure and joy,
no matter the outcome in the end.
So many questions to be asked,
without the words to put them in.

What was the connection, for instance,
between the mitre box in the basement used
for cutting clean edges that will match
on the diagonal, and the mitre box
where we dropped our pennies—
our 'mites'—"for the poor pagan babies"?
Who those "pagan babies" might be,
and whether pagans were always poor,
were questions beyond the asking.

The wondering is the seam, the join,
you see, between then and now.
Between who we were and who
we're still becoming:
the space most in need of
tending and attending to.

Like all builders, poets need
to build their structures true:
straight, and on the level.
But with seams still visible.

If they aren't, we'll become
like Beckett's Chas, who
having lost a harrow,
finds a figure of speech instead.

May the poetry gods spare us that.
May the planing of our poems
to plain speech ensure it.

✎ LANGUAGE ACQUISITION

Her nose doesn't reach the top of the bassinet,
but she knows a new baby is sleeping inside.
Her three-year-old brain knows she's on her own now.
She has no word for that yet.
        That word is *self-reliance.*

Making her rounds three summers later,
climbing the steep steps to concrete-block porches,
she takes her place beside another old man:
Mr. Kibble, Mr. Guilford, Mr. Dunkelbarger.
Each one's long slatted porch swing glides
slowly back and forth, creaky as the voice
unspooling the history of his working life:
of the store owned; the tools sold
after leaving the shop, still missed,
maybe more than the wife he's lost.

Listening, gazing at her own house
across the street, she knows
all the meaning there is
is in the silence, and in the mingled
smell of ancient flesh, pipe tobacco,
and burnt toast.
        Contentment is the word here.

Bored with pushing another new baby,
she's caught executing sidewalk wheelies
with the stroller for the amusement
of the neighborhood boys.
The spanking administered in front of them
requires another word she doesn't yet have.
        Humiliation would be that word.

Tending other peoples' babies before long,
terrified by the creakings in a strange house,
knowing nothing about babies, or the fathers
who drive her home through dark streets,
their whiskey-and-lighter-fluid breath
filling the car and her nostrils,
in time she'll learn the words for that too:
  male sexual desire.

Escaping to the woods, she paddles
her father's canoe over the waters
of the Maumee and Auglaize.
The sound of her oars echoes off
the arches of the dark, cobwebbed
viaduct: a remnant of the Erie Canal.
The stories of the ancient ones echo
off the walls too. She feels the presence
of those whose dugouts had paddled
the same waters:
  Shawnee, Wyandotte, Ottawa,
    Chippewa, Wea, Potawatomi,
     Delaware, Miami.

Her word-horde grows in biology class.
She learns each blade of grass has a spine.
Thirsty, it closes in on itself, like a book.
Sated, it opens wide again. As she does,
opening to the words in the books
she studies, learning that everything living
fits into its proper place:
  domain, kingdom, phylum, class,
    order, family, genus,
     species, variety.

Her woods-roaming starts to take on
purpose and passion. Classifying leaves
of the gingko, collecting praying mantis pupas;
storing them in the laundry room cupboard.
In the warmth and darkness there they break open,
hundreds of tiny mantises flying around the room
when the cupboard door is opened,
vexing her mother; delighting her.
But what was the classification
she belonged to? A fish out of water:
　　　Devonian tetrapodomorpha?

Hungering for the tactile, not the tactical,
resigned to being consigned to the secretarial track.
But she hungers, oh, for the light:
for the outdoors; for the sun;
　　　for the sweet paw paw's juice,
　　　　　the mango, the gingko,
　　　　　　　the papaya, the pine.

The generosity of others releases her
into the local college. There will be
no pearls or Pendletons there.
Living at home, growing in sophistication,
she recognizes the operative word now has
three meanings. That word is
　　　accommodation.

Children who are coddled, some say,
grow up to discover they've been sent to the Arctic
with a map of the Italian lakes.
But her history has left her
arriving instead at every
Italian lake still clutching
　　　a detailed map
　　　　　of the Arctic.

☙ FIRST CONFESSION

The white Necco wafers worked perfectly.
Just slip into Church during recess
and play First Communion. It was
practice, not parody, though
Sister Consolata didn't seem to agree.

First Confession will be the place,
we are told, to ask for forgiveness
and begin doing penance. But at seven,
what could we possibly have done wrong?
Not even the small thing: the "venial."

It was Rummert who sinned, I knew.
Never showing up where his place
had been set for supper, but hiding
his peas under his plate all the same.
Or caroming wildly on the backyard
swing, requiring that he be smacked hard.
Punished. Taught a lesson.

The Necco wafer Communion Caper
would turn out to be our *second* sin.
We knew the first one we were about
to confess would be the lie concocted
in the confessional: a made-up transgression
confessed in lieu of a sin, because
without that, what would there be to tell?

Better it would have been had there been
two confessionals: one where our lies
could be confessed; another, where the
burden of sins committed against us
might be laid down, and left behind.

ᔕ STEAMY MESSAGES

Our mother's arm passed back and forth
over the ironing board, pressing
steamy messages into our underpants,
her attention divided between the ironing,
and the latest adventures of Cynthia, as
The Romance of Helen Trent wafted
from the radio sitting atop the fridge.

In her basement's coolness blocks away,
Grandma Ollie is doing the same,
steam rising over the priests' boxer shorts
and sheets she irons, folding each piece
neatly into the oval wicker basket before
delivering them to the parish house.

Her quiet work will buy her a ramshackle cottage
by the river where she plays cards,
shares a beer or two with her lady friends
and ladles stew from the
pot simmering on her stove.

But no money, property, or pleasure accrues to
our mother pressing her steamy messages
into our underpants.
Walking to school, our cheeks
absorb those steamy messages:
Be wrinkle-free.
Learn to type, and to apologize.
We soon learn to do both,
at eighty words a minute.

The micrometer in Dad's shirt pocket is used
to set up machines making munitions and parts
for use in the war effort.

It calibrates miniscule distances,
but proves useless for measuring
the ones in his wife's moods.

Sitting at the kitchen table at shift's end,
steam rising from his four o'clock coffee,
he presses his own steamy messages
onto his children:
"Don't let no one shit on you.
Open yer mouth."

Maybe it was "speak up" he meant.
But we suspected a less savory possibility.
Confronted with a new rule to be followed,
a new necessity that needed to be bought
and somehow paid for, he only shook his head
and sighed that, well, once again,
he'd just have to peel it and eat it,
since you could just never win fer losin'.

We listened, watched, absorbed.
Took up the heavy burden of
keeping things light.
Learned to laugh at failure.
Steeling ourselves to fail,
neatly and quietly,
so we would have something
to laugh at.

Working hard all our lives
to keep the "laughing" part,
peeling and eating only what was
unchangeable, working even harder
at losing the "can't win fer losin" part.

ᔐ MANUAL LABOR, MAXIMAL LOVE

It was skill and love that built the desk.
The three coats of varnish transforming
its particle board top into a fine shining surface
       proved that.

So did the old Olivetti sitting on it,
found somehow for the daughter
the kindness of others was sending to college.
She and the Olivetti come to life there,
tapping out essays in the five a.m. quiet.

Below, the sounds of her father
shuffling up the basement stairs
after shoveling coal into the furnace
to put on the work clothes suffused
with the sweet smell of machine oil.

She listens; knows whatever power
she wields is over a machine too:
responding as the vibrator raises
the Olivetti's ribbon and the type bars
in its center well rise at her fingers'
commands, imprinting paper
carefully rolled onto its platen.
No carriage return until *she* hears the 'ding';
no response but to *her* hand sweeping up
to make the carriage return return.
No matter that the margins of each letter
typed were a bit furred and blurry.
       So were her own.

Setting margins meant different things.
Monday to Saturday, 3:30 to 6 and
Sundays all day during tax season.

She sets margins to be filled with figures
at the CPA's office, transforming
grocery bags stuffed with rumpled receipts
for hot dog buns, and register tapes from
restaurants and roadhouses into
spread sheet columns: *In-coming; out-going.*
Categories already beginning to shape her.

At home, spread sheets involve lace curtains,
spread every Spring in the sun in the side yard
on stretchers lined with finishing nails holding
the curtains in place while they dry,
to be released, nail by nail, with an audible
       sprong.

Curtain stretchers, type wells, ribbon vibrators—
all gone now, along with her Dad's brace and bit,
and Uncle Vincent, whose clothes were suffused
with the delicious smells of his shoe repair shop
echoing always with the low growl of grinders;
the high whine of lathes.

His singing echoing too, ricocheting around
the old car he drove each weekend to the acres
where the house he was all alone building
for his family was rising, bit by slow bit.
His five daughters crammed in the back seat
on the way to help him build it.
They, whining and protesting, he becoming
a swingin' Rosemary Clooney, singing

"Come on-a my house, my house a-come-on,"
       all the way there.

WHISTLING WHILE YOU WORK

> The first thing I do when I get a book on
> prehistoric man is go to the index to see
> whether it has the word "play." You find
> Plato but not "play." Yet, whenever we try
> to trace the origin of skill, we usually reach
> the realm of play.
>
> Eric Hoffer, in *First Things, Last Things.*

Play made Hoffer's work on the waterfront go faster.
His play was wonderful words, leaving his hands free
to do the job at hand, furnishing and entertaining his
mind at the same time.

Working people know this. That's why their play
includes whistling, and the kind of wordplay
found in the best poets. Useful for passing the time.
For the working man, safe too:
beyond the hearing range of foremen,
and, frequently, cautionary.

Like that joke passed around the shop,
shared with every new guy coming on shift.
The one showing how the punch press operator
sitting on the bar stool orders four beers.
He holds up two fingers. The two he still has.

Or a tall Dad, bonking his head on a low basement
pipe, assuring his kids wincing in sympathy,
"Don't worry, it's only my head!" Or on his knees,
his long frame squeezing itself behind the toilet
to find the pesky leak, looking over his shoulder
to tell his children with an exaggerated faux sigh:

"A man in my position!"

KITCHEN TABLE

Where the banjos and guitars get played.
Where spoons are brought out for making rhythm,
not for feeding face.
The big bowl of chips does that.

Where neighbor comes to sit and talk.
Where unwinding at shift's end happens.
Where pattern and material are spread out
before cutting.

Where jokes are shared, problems hashed out,
slights and insults retracted, relived, rehashed;
lost friends or family remembered.

Second option, in season: picnic table.
Must be wood, rectangular, built by hand.
Extreme care must be taken swinging legs
under crossbar before sitting down.
Bolts there can cause
a wicked gouge in a leg.

Care must also be taken
to be sure an equal number
of bodies of approximately
the same size and weight sit
on each side or it tips over,
taking with it the bowl of potato salad,
ketchup bottle, mustard jar—

the whole shebang.

∾ DREAM WORK

It is almost eight years since I retired
from the waterfront, but in my dreams
I still load and unload ships....One might
maintain that a pension is pay for the work
we keep on doing after we retire.

        Eric Hoffer, in "Works and Days"

Set-up men probably reached into their pajama pocket
feeling for their micrometer, checking one last time
that their set-up was accurate for the order.

The factory foremen probably walked
the factory floors through the night,
making sure their workers were working
at optimal speed; were sober and safe.

The legs of their wives probably twitched
under their blankets as they chased a
misbehaving child running through the woods.
Or their fingers twitched as they dreamed
of twisting the neck of another chicken
destined to be tomorrow's supper.

My own fingers still twitch through the night,
typing the dialogue going on in my dreams.
Or I wake exhausted from a night spent
trying to explain something to students,
and not succeeding. In a happier version,
walking into class on a new term's opening day
bearing a bowl of apples, their aroma filling the room
as I shuffle toward my desk in puffy pink slippers,
hoping, I guess, to comfort that way
the new batch of learners.

APRICOT TREE

No one in the family liked apricots,
though it just could be that we'd
never eaten one that hadn't fallen
on the ground, a mushy,
over-ripe mess
with bees swarming
all over it.

But to cut it down? Maybe it was because
too many not yet ripe hard ones kept
dropping onto the roof, keeping us
awake at night.
Was that reason enough?

Or was it a father's need to just, well,
be doing something decisive:
something not ordered or overseen
by a shop foreman.

Or maybe it was just the desire to
rid us of one more thing in which
taste failed to measure up
to what its smell promised.
Few things ever do.

That must've been it.

❧ ODE TO DICK CLARK

Run-Around Sue. Little Richard
in tight pants and pompadour
with the gal named Sue.
The Everly Brothers trying to Wake Up
their Little Susie who'd fallen asleep
after the loving was a bit more plausible,
but then maybe we only thought so
because we'd been seduced by those ducktails.
We suspected as much,
we Susies, Sues, Suzys and Susans,
all of us now of an age.

We may have been busy on the dance floor
or in the back seat, but we also recognized
the war going on: a war of bland white music,
its major weapon gentle persuasion passing
for whimsy, and a dollop or more of repression.
We knew that. So did Dick Clark.
Sure, he offered up plenty pretty white boys—
the Crew Cuts, ShBoom-ing.

But when The Ames Brothers tried to convince us
there might be such a thing as a Naughty Lady
on Shady Lane, we didn't buy it. I mean, four
white guys who had a hit named "Rag Mop"?
The Shirelles' "Will you Still Love Me Tomorrow"
was more plausible, mostly because the word
naughty, a word we knew parents only
used on toddlers, wasn't in the lyrics.

But we were patient. Kept waiting for you
to start giving us access to some real music.
Plus, we needed to watch the dancers
so we could learn the stroll, and some
antidote to the fare on evening TV.

The faux insouciance of Perry Como's "Hot Diggity."
Or Pat Boone, sounding like everybody's Dad.

Even Theresa Brewer's plea to "Let Me Go Lover"
was just another stab at speaking to our fear
of being stuck here—maybe for the rest of our lives.
This some of us, at least, suspected.

We just weren't buying the Unchained Melody
lyrics any more than we were Patti's cutesy inquiry
into the price of that Doggie in the Window.

And forget all those portly, mostly white guys
pretending to Rock Around the Clock.
We may have been white, but we knew what
a real rhythm with a back beat could do.
It was nothing like what was being hammered
on the piano, except for Jerry Lee Lewis of course.

In the end it was the royalty—Gene Chandler's
Duke of Earl, and The Imperials, we waited for.
Especially Little Anthony: small, with a too-big
mouth and a heart-wrenching androgynous voice.

The Tears on his Pillow were ours too: his face and
voice, the antidote to what the culture, the music
industry, or just the '50s, was trying to foist off on
restless teens not living in hip Philly, a place where
we knew groups were sharpening their harmonies
in row house doorways, while we were locked
in the land-locked Midwest,
already looking for a way out.

If the music had to be white, we decided,
let it be made by those Philly guys.
Black restlessness and passion in a white frame,
like Dion and the Belmonts, maybe. You knew this.

◇ SHIFTING GEARS: TOOLS OF THE TRADE

> Strange to be ignorant of how things work.
>
> Philip Larkin, in "Ignorance"

Larkin mostly meant seeds bursting through soil:
the kind of thing Thomas Hardy knew so well:
landscapes degged with dew, full of flitches of fern
spied in the thawing brume.

But what of our ignorance of *other* word-hordes,
and of the people who have, use, and live them?
Orbital sanders, flanges, sprockets, awls, augers,
capacitors, not to mention EDMs and CNCs,
Electrical Discharge Machines and Computer
Numerical Controls, or the micrometers they replaced.

The tools of the trade shift with the times, the needs,
and the job at hand: the thing being built, measured,
cobbled together, repaired, re-imagined, repurposed,
shorn up or torn down: a frame, a cupboard,
      a friendship, a life.

Take *shift* just for instance:
Seven to four, unless you worked the night shift.
Dinner was meat and potatoes eaten,
say, from 11:30 to noon: at shift break.
Lunch was a word never heard, though the word
shiftless was. It had begun as a kindly word, in 1562,
the OED tells us: "Wylde beastes be cruel,
yet God defends the shiftles sheepe."
But from the start there was a wrestling for its
meaning. Earliest, being shiftless had nothing to do
with being a restless, no-good lay-about.

Shift your eyes from an old OED to the latest.
The negatives outnumber and dominate:
"helpless, lacking cunning or artifice; lacking
resourcefulness, initiative, or ambition; lazy,
inefficient, incompetent; ineffective, futile."
Only at the end, the earliest use appears:
"lacking a shift or shirt."

You see how a word-horde can be a tool.
It produces in me embarrassment at needing
to ask a knowledgeable worker to fix something.
Lacking the right tools, we feel shiftless. Useless.

Word-hordes are a part of what keep us
from going where we might want to go.
Shape how we see ourselves, and others.
They are tools, and sometimes weapons.
They tell each of us where we "belong,"
and where we don't; where we're welcome,
         and where we're not.

We style shift to lay claim to space, rank, place.
We might describe our ancestors for instance
as taciturn and peripatetic, or as folks
who spoke little, and moved a lot.

Cape Cod newcomers will know they're being
sized up by the Oldcomers until they learn
bayside means along old 6A, and *backside,*
the places hugging Nantucket Sound,
just as Native Hawaiians, asked for directions,
will tell you to go *Mauka*, toward the mountains,
         or *Makai,* toward the sea.

So many places to go and ways to get there.
         Words fail me.

➷ HEAVEN AT THE CLUB ONE-ELEVEN

> I like bars close to home and home run down,
> a signal to the world I'm weak.

> Richard Hugo, in "The Hilltop"

A slow Wednesday night.
Neon in the windows
announces *Schlitz, Diehl's, Blatz.*
Throws a glow on the silver
Airstream Esther lives in,
parked just to the left
of her roadhouse.
A lozenge lying on its side
lighting the way inside,
and the river across the road.

Inside, the sound of crunch of tires
on gravel gives Esther her signal
to start mixing a pink lady or
a white Russian. We've been
poring over mixology books
lately, sampling things
we've never heard of.

I sip, and struggle to join the chatter
of the old German farmers parked
on the stools beside my own:
"weary proletarians at rest
on arse and elbow,"
Beckett's Belacqua calls them.
Me, I just hope some genetic memory
will give me a leg up
on the language.

Maybe, I think, I can tap a bit of
the lingo and gusto of
the great grandpa whose
fiddle is still riddled with
half-moon grooves marking
where his fingernails rapped out
the rhythm at hoedowns in houses
where rugs were pulled up to
make space for the dance.
Buck dancing, clogging, flat-footing,
neighbors lining up for a Virginia reel,
no doubt.

But it's his passion more than his music I want.
Maybe a bit of his anger too:
anger at losing his farm and his home;
anger at being forced into factory work
way past his sixty-fifth year.

Esther supplies some of that too.
Sliding a second pink lady across the bar
and a glance in my direction,
she lets drop that my husband-to-be
has been parking on my stool nights
he's working late and I'm not here,
his ear cocked for the honk
of one particular car
slow-driving by,
signaling a tryst is on tap.

CONVERSION THERAPY

Fortunately the saucers had rims.
They were what saved the pooling ice cream
and the soggy cake swimming in it from
a spill-over on the kitchen table.
The priest and the girl he was sent
to reason back to belief were
too busy to notice the meltdown.
He, earnestly talking of girlfriends
he'd given up, including the one
who'd admired his shell-pink ears,
while she wondered silently what that
had to do with her questions, like
why anyone could want to endure
for all eternity; how anyone could not see
that it's life's ephemerality that inspires
our most intense attention, appreciation,
       and joy.

What had only ever consoled were the rituals:
the Latin, the incense, and finally,
only a father's little finger curling lovingly
around her own on the pew as they stood
side-by-side, mid-Mass.

That, and later, the way the ornate doors
shut out the hum, fumes,
and bits of glass fiber wafting over
from the Johns Manville factory
across the street, shutting out those things,
and all the sounds of everyday chatter too:
about the price of hamburger,
the latest fashion trends.

Reverence requires no more
than a long, quiet walk in the woods.

∾ LOLLIPOPS

Invited to join the professors'
private evening reading group
discussing the latest Updike novel,
the precocious undergrad protests:
"But ordinary people don't *have* affairs!"
The professors smile, cryptically.

Lollipops, their wives called the co-eds,
smart enough to be mildly interesting;
too naive to see they were prey.

How many of them experienced the trysts
in weedy fields, driven there in small
foreign cars unfamiliar in a GM town,
their interiors suffused with the smell
of Gallois. Each car's owner, a river otter
eager to rut in the muck and tall grass.
Or mosquitoes lured to their targets
by the smell of butyric acid on skin.

True, it was a bit of a two-way street.
The hunters, smart enough to be
 mildly interesting to the hunted,
 though the seduction poems slipped
 into the notebooks of the prey
 were sub-standard and, the hunted
 suspected, frequently recycled.

The hunters presumed their fine minds
were the bait. It was not so.
Not even when it was the randy Ayn Rand fan
testing the limits of his John Galt self.
His exceptional right, he presumed,
to flummox small town girls.

✌ THE SIMINDINGER BABY

Little sister, you were and still are Beebo or Beebs,
the baby sister in thrice handed down hand-me-downs.
Lucky for your older sisters,
Aunt Mary Alice had always been stylin'.

But mostly, you got nothing handed down,
every piece plain worn out, faded, or ragged
by the time it was your turn.
Our stash of photos proves that.
You, the bottom stair step in our crew
until baby brother Mook came along.
No Easter bonnet sat jaunty on your head.
Instead, just a faded head scarf.
You were the sweet-faced Babushka child.

Your heart leapt not long ago to discover
a photo of you as an infant.
A rarity for the third baby, especially
if it was just another girl, so "ho hum," right?

Happy to find that one photo, you turned it over
to discover, written in our father's hand,
a notation. "The Simindinger Baby," it said.
A final, painful, indignity.
He'd not recognized you as his own.

We laugh now, knowing he loved you dearly.
But I can tell the hurt still lurks.
We ease it by giving one another
yet another nickname. Until a better one
comes along, you will be for me
"the Simindinger Baby," TSB for short,
and I, TSBS.

II

DANCER'S CHOICE

Dancer Gelsey Kirkland had her lips
injected with silicone to approximate
the look of a dancer whose face
Balanchine admired.

Taught to be taut,
to turn out in
perfect, exquisite pain,
the dancer first feigns,
then feels,
abandon,
knowing the alternative
   to be
      the slow
        tap
         dance
           away.

Before being taught,
in the beginning, words.
To abandon
the taut word,
its fierce precision a
necessary beauty,
abandoning art,
   is to begin
      the slow
        tap
         dance
           awry.

ꙮ SOBBING ACROSS OKLAHOMA

It was hardly the trail of tears, though
before the ink on the marriage certificate
was dry, it produced many during the
ride in that '64 Chevy convert to El Paso's
Fort Bliss, a name by now her literary training
allows her to find ironic,
but her heart, far less so.

A year and more of Texas borderland
sand and the dusty streets of Ciudad Juarez.
They were as one town, still available
to both Mexicans, and gringos like her.

The beautiful faces, and the names she wrote
in her grade book seemed to tell
the whole history of Mexico:
Carmen Acevez' dark eyes,
beautifully Mayan. Those of
Maria de los Angeles Arronte,
blue-eyed and beautifully Spanish.

All of us speaking an easy Chamizal Spanish:
"Dónde està the bobby pins?" in the salon;
"Andale!" on the way to the restaurant for
some food, "Muy caliente."

✑ EL PASO TO JUAREZ AND BACK, 1965

Roll down the window at the border
so the head stretching into the car
can cast a quick look,
eyes sweeping across our faces.
We call out breezily: "Just a
couple more gringos heading over
for some good food."
Sated and a bit tipsy.
Coming back,
same story.

Juarez's dusty brick main street
lined with restaurants; filled
with gringos like us. Waiters
handsome, friendly, languid.
Food plentiful; drinks strong.
No shot glasses: just a
generous pour.

Now the generous pour has
slowed. Over the border, too,
with its sensors, barbed wire,
and chunks of concrete
"repurposed" from fortresses
in the Middle East.

Fifty years on, it's clear
not everything improves
with time.

✺ THE FAIRIES SING BACK IN OHIO

The three sisters stand hip to haunch
in the crepuscular living room light
as they always had when he'd
asked them to sing, or to line up
in the yard for the annual holiday
or mid-summer photo. Six, nine, twelve.
Matching harlequin pedal pushers,
triangles of green, red, and yellow
covering six skinny legs.

Facing his own long legs they'd
squinted in the sun as they'd
squinted at the Chesterfield King
dangling from his lower lip.

Now the spindly legs are his,
crossed at the ankles as he sits in his
recliner next to the amber ashtray,
useless and empty now.

First one, then another sister begins
to sing: "White coral bells,
upon a slender stalk..."
Their voices thinner,
more tentative, even,
than back then.

Their Changeable now loveable Charlie
furrows a brow. Smiles.

NUTS AND BOLTING, 1967

Baby in the backseat, radio blaring,
plastic baby bottle melted by the heat
of the car's cigarette lighter
heaved out the window
into a passing cornfield.

On her way, in the driver's seat this time,
headed to anywhere but there. There,
where the husband's new job required
she be introduced to the boss.

She'd sat sobbing in the parking lot.
Unable to play the part of the little woman.
She'd endured even before the wedding
a plague of nightmares: bodies in coffins
"on exhibit" at the Guggenheim.
Visitors walking up the ramp,
pausing to study each of those bodies,
each one part of a living diorama,
each one in each diorama exhibiting
a different stage
of decomposition,
each one still breathing.

Endured Freudian slips by day,
"attended church" becoming
"attempted church" in what she read.

Knowing something better or at least other
had to be out there somewhere.
Smart enough to know when and how
to bolt, thaw frozen pipes without help,
find the nearest Home Depot,
buy the blowtorch to thaw them,
and her own heart.

III

ELIDIN' N' RIDIN'

Yer ridin' fer a fall girl, ridin' fer a fall.
but ridin' n' fallin's better'n
not ridin' at all.

✌ FOREVER VIETNAM

From Beaver Cleaver to Eldridge Cleaver,
a long distance. Even longer,
from Dominic Savio to Mario Savio.

Martin was going door to door in Cambridge,
asking at each one, "Will you walk with me?"
Maybe he had no time to stop at every door.
Or maybe he saw the poster in the front window:
the one with the fist in black power salute,
so he moved on.

The first memory of the baby in that apartment
 was of marching in protests
            through Harvard Square.

He wouldn't be a witness to some of the worst.
Or the best: the dancing in the streets when
LBJ announced he "would not seek,"
and "would not accept" a second term.

But that war was far from over.
Maybe it never will be.
The yoga class still includes a
tunnel rat whose lived experiences
the rest of us can barely imagine.

The hyper-alert vets in classrooms
still make sure to sit in the back row,
prepared to leap over desks
at the sound of every fire alarm.
The brilliant man at the shelter
still hoists the stumps of both legs
to the table top to be comfortable talking
about his favorite poet: Tennyson, whose
Ulysses says "I am a part of all that I have met."

✑ MY LAST LEPIDOPTERA

"Let me show you my favorite butterfly. I was walking
in the woods, and it just flew right into my hand."
I was no particular lover of butterflies, but this one—it
wasn't only that it was beautiful, but it—well, I guess I
came to love it because it could fly, and I couldn't."

"I tore a page from an old book, folded it around the
butterfly, put it in my shirt pocket and took it home,
where I grew more and more fond of pulling it out of
the pocket—just to look at it, you know."

"One day I pulled back the drapes, held it up to the
light—just to study and admire the spots on its wings.
Sometimes I tested myself. Tried to remember their
pattern without taking it out of my pocket. I could do
it, too. Remember every spot and fleck. Soon, I
couldn't leave the house without tapping my chest to
be sure it was still there."

"One day I noticed the spots seemed to be changing.
Not dramatically, you know, but one time I'd look at it
and it would look the same. The next time I checked, I
was sure it was changing. A new spot forming here or
there, or an old one, spreading like spilt soup on a
tablecloth. Sometimes, even seeming to fade before
my gaze. I couldn't ignore all that, could I?"

"I found myself looking at it more and more closely,
turning it this way and that. I discovered it wasn't hard
to just pinch the strange spots out with my fingernails.
If I did it gently, I could barely see the hole. I did this
for a long time. Every day, checking to assure myself
it still looked the same, and when it didn't, restoring it
by the method I describe...."

∽ VENUS AND MARS

Stunningly beautiful, statuesque,
with an aquiline nose. Accomplished,
as they say, in a hundred ways:
musically talented, multilingual.
Self-sufficient.

But sitting across from me
in the diner, a sorry sight.
Red-eyed, hunched over,
clutching a crumpled Kleenex.

The latest lover was heading
back to California to the wife
he swore he'd left. "Forever."
Heading back because, he'd explained,
"She needs me."

Reaching for a consoling response,
I can't stop thinking instead of one
of the top ten selling self-help books
of the last 25 years. The one I hated.

Men, its author said, are motivated
by being needed; women, he said,
when they are cherished.

What could I say to my friend?
That her self-reliance was her undoing?
I can't remember what I said:
remember only that wordlessly
she threw her crumpled Kleenex
in my direction.

ꙮ LOVE

> Whenever I tried to sing of love,
> it turned to pain. And again, when
> I tried to sing of pain, it turned
> to love.
>
> Franz Schubert

Being nomadic, the parting lovers
have only psychic furniture to divide.

They hug decades-old slights tight,
preferring them to any other embrace.

He chooses the wry shrug;
she, the tapping foot.
He, the furtive glance;
she, the heavy sigh.

His, the half-smile the eyes belie,
the absent stare.

Hers, the pained look, steady glare,
the clipped response,
the look away.

His, the narrowed eyes,
the faux-surprised step back.

Hers, the turn on the heel,
the walk away.

✎ TRANSPARENCY

Had there been any giggles, gasps,
or campus gendarmes as that girl
walked along the street on
her way to her professor's office?

That was the first question
dropping itself into my brain
as my eyes dropped to the chest
of the girl sitting across from his desk,
fixing on the two brown nipples
covered only by the sheerest of fabric.
The eyes dropped, while the head
said "stop making sense,"
so she did.

She'd dropped by just to say hello.
Was in the neighborhood.
That was why she'd dropped by;
how her eyes had come to land
where they did; how her mind
had come to puzzle so.

Had there been some jacket
thrown over the back of her chair
during that office visit?

There just must have been
a jacket, she decided,
heading home.
A jacket. That must've been it.

ᕲ TOM

His body had risen up to kill him
because beneath him there was no
earth where the soul could stand.

Frank Bidart, in "The Lightning
Across an Open Field"

Is there a word for the preternatural thing
beyond talent or skill? You had that.
The gospel singers glide from table to table
at the Sunday brunch in Midtown,
handing off their mics to mouths full of
mimosa, French toast, and eggs bennie.
A bemused singer hands one to you.
As one, the whole place stops chewing
and sipping, and sucks in breath.

What came out of your mouth, skinny,
Minnesota blonde boy-man, was no reedy
quaver. Close eyes, and every ear in the house
heard the deep sound of the Mississippi delta,
every nostril filling with the smell of
workers' sweat, and the hot, reedy shore.

They hadn't listened, as I had for years,
to you on the mouth-harp; you on the guitar,
you singing, or reading from your poems,
most often whimsical, John Ashbery-like.
They hadn't watched you transform
ratty apartments in Hell's Kitchen, Alphabet City,
or Dinky Town into habitable spaces.

Magic and *Tragic* should not rhyme.
You really were "a creative,"
as they say in the ad biz.

But you were more than that.
So much more
than your Don Draper day job
        could hold.

The one you held onto as long as you could,
though, alas, not without the aid of Adderall,
tranqs, and the booze that kept you afloat—
        until it pulled you under.

KINETIC ART

for Tom

I walked around your legs carefully,
but stumbled over them anyway.
Picking myself up, walking around
the body the legs held up
I pushed, poked—here, there.
Where it looked soft
I pushed with a finger,
expecting at least an indentation,
or maybe a hole that would fill itself up
with itself while I walked away.

But the soft spots weren't ever where I thought—
or else they kept migrating.
Some places looked hard until, astounded,
I watched while they turned amoebic,
flowing over my foot,
swallowing it whole.

With my free foot, I gave you a nudge.
Later, I pushed. Hard.
You didn't budge.
Giving up, walking away,
out of the corner of my eye
I caught your leap and snicker.

They came, I think, from one of those soft spots.

NIGHT MOVES: HAWAII

Inside,
temperature drops,
then rises.
Egg descends.
Turning the page
of her book,
she curls closer to
her cat.
Outside,
tom cat sniffs,
howls.

In the dream she'd said
"No more,
you've been wonderful but...."
He'd cried, then convened a party.
All her friends there.
Food tumbling from bowls:
silver, porcelain, crystal, pottery, glass.

In the kitchen, an irregular silky star
of spilled milk spreads over the floor,
glittering shards of glass floating
in the translucent star.

Kneeling, she sucks up
milk and glass together,
holding all, delicately,
in her mouth.

﹏ GEMINI

The half of you not wanted
came swimming up,
up through the tiny hole in
a circle of convulsing rubber
where it met your other,
wanted half, and you became.
Became, knew, and grew used
to being the one wanted and not wanted;
wanting and not; wanton and not.
Half female courage—diving down,
half male—riding surfaces, sailing waves:
androgyne, tacking towards the depths.

﹏ RUNNERS RUNNING

His, the solid footfalls on dried and curling leaves,
his steady exhalations whispering his demons
into the crotches of naked trees where he knows
the orphaned child will wait for him to pass:
today, tomorrow, and forever.

Her slower steps shuffle her demons
into the mudded spaces between uneven bricks
where they wait, mute as his, pressing
sometimes instead into the rotting guavas
as she climbs her mountain to that waterfall
where she will stand trying once more
to wash away her own burden,
as alone and unshared as his.

ᔐ ALPHABET CITY:
EAST 10TH, BETWEEN C AND D

The cabbie asks, "Are you sure?"
I say yes. We head for the loft
with narrow stairs the word
rickety was meant for.
Dust clings to the loft's raw floors
where miscellaneous machines, saws and
a trash-picked couch sits rumpled and worn.
An ancient fridge rumbles in a corner.

The next morning, at the New York Public,
the catalog was catnip.
That's CATNYP— Catalogue of the NY Public,
of course. Librarians have a sense of humor.

In the Berg Collection I sit,
turning over and reading some of the
14,000 Dickens letters now scattered
over several continents.
"I'm tired of all this..." one says, ending
mid-sentence. He'd run to the end
of his piece of paper.

Across the way at the Pierpont Morgan,
inside a shoebox labeled "Miscellaneous
Autographs, British," an envelope is found,
bearing the Inimitable's handwriting,
and the right date. At the tip of the triangle
on its inside flap
is one word:
Rot.

IV

"Throw your heart down here"

Sung by banjo players in Africa as captives
were being driven onto ships headed for the
Americas. A banjo player onboard a slave ship
meant more people would survive the journey.

Related by Abigail Washburn, in
conversation with Krista Tippett and
banjo players Washburn and Béla Fleck
aired on PBS's "On Being."

❧ CHECKING IN AT HOTEL DIEU

It was the perfect marriage for a therapist
to parse: the alcoholic son, full of anger
at his teacher-mother for banishing
his philandering, alcoholic doctor father
marries the daughter of parents
whose clear but unspoken message
had been that her survival depended
on her own resources, including the option
that she become a teacher.

One year into the marriage, she is carrying
a small suitcase into Hotel Dieu.
Inside it is no beachwear or cocktail dress.
Instead, a yellow dotted-swiss nightgown
and a few toiletries.

She has no idea why a hospital
is named Hotel Dieu, but she knows
without a doubt she's in labor.
Knows—and is far from surprised—
that her husband has wordlessly dropped
her off at the curb at its front entrance
and driven away.
It's a long walk up that sidewalk.
At its end, she checks herself in.

She's also not surprised days later
when he's not appeared to drive her home.
Not appeared to meet his newborn son.
She'd already been contemplating a taxi.
Is surprised when he appears. Suspects
it was her furious doctor who'd called him.

No matter, really. She'd had the candy-stripers,
most of them her students, for company.

She's finally begun to recognize that she's a
surrogate target for her husband's anger,
an insight offering small consolation
as she walks to the end of the quiet corridor
each night to gaze at the only gringo baby
in the nursery. Hers, of course.
Standing at its long window
she gazes long at her sleeping son,
whispering apologies
to the sweet face
before it even has a name.

Turning to gaze out the window
behind her at El Paso's low mountains
in the distance, she struggles
to imagine a future for the two of them
she has no energy yet to imagine.

✍ TRACKS

A single person is missing for you, and
the whole world is empty, but one no
longer has the right to say so aloud.

Philippe Arias, in *Western Attitudes
Toward Death*

The eye of the girl who grew up along the tracks
is now tracking the ophthalmologist's
finger tracking her eye's macular degeneration.
The indifferent macula pay no mind, drusen
floating lazily, muscae volitantes drifting
right or left with her gaze
like a canoe on Flax Pond,
or humunculi in pond water.

Tracking these musings, she drifts back
again to his degeneration—to the tracks
on his arm, as he, too, drifted farther away,
until he could find no way back home:
no more his fault than the drusen are hers.

Driving home, sunglasses protecting
dilated pupils, she thinks of the ones
he wore to protect his eyes from her
anxious gaze, and then, of how frustrating
it is in older age to be expected to see the world
more clearly just as vision fades;
to keep track of struggles in the newspapers
—the devastation and the poverty—just as eyes
have begun to see every line of type double.
To listen with care and full attention
to the stories of others' struggles
just as hearing fades.

～ "KNOW YE"

First two words of the Certificate of Small Estates
in the Surrogate's Court of the County of New York.

A day before, she'd found herself flexing the knee
of one leg back and forth against a step on the stairs
leading to her front door, her other leg rigid against
the concrete walkway. Waiting for her son to call
from the road to say he would be home soon.
She was reading a detective novel.

When the call came, it would be a detective:
Detective Schenk. NYPD. 7th Precinct,
        Lower East Side.
Telephone to her ear, knee still flexing,
she was already davening. "Car crash?"
was what came out of her mouth, but
she already knew the answer was otherwise.

Allen Street. Slumped over his steering wheel.
Needle still in his arm, she would be told.
The next day, she'd learn one doesn't
identify a body, as CSI viewers might assume.
Instead, in the basement morgue a photo is slid
across a small round table in a small room
for her to see. What she saw was her son's
        peaceful smile.

She'd mention that later, after she'd
collected the empty wallet in the basement
of City Hall; signed the papers testifying
that yes, she was mother of that cadaver
with the beatific smile. Detective Schenk laughed:
"Of course! He was high!"
He'd meant no harm.

The words had just tumbled out at South Station:
"I'm going to pick up my son's body."
A caramel-colored hand reached through the space
under the ticket-counter grate and stroked hers,
a soft, caramel voice whispering, "I'm so sorry."

A kindness, like that of the portly young man
running the storefront mortuary. From her pallet
on West 160th, she'd listened late into the night
to salsa wafting from high windows outside.
In the morning he'd gently draw a faded curtain
across the back half of his one-room mortuary,
shielding her and the cardboard coffin from
the busyness of the street.

Stroking those beautiful, cold chiseled cheeks,
she wondered how that perfect body
could already be emitting the smells
of putrefaction, as it floated and lurched
from side to side in its bed of melting ice.

"Saying our goodbyes" never applies.
We keep saying them, years later:
years after watching the rusting
white Ford Econoline van bear away—
No, say it: *drove* away—on its way
to an incinerator in New Jersey.

Outside, overhead, the window of the
homeward-bound Amtrak framed
white clouds in a cerulean sky.
Inside, overhead, a suitcase,
a small box inside.

 There is no heaven
 but memory.

RUE FOR REMEMBRANCE

All things are cured by salt:
either sweat, or tears, or the sea.

Isak Dinesen

Victorian ladies' books named rue
the flower for remembrance.
Planted in late June, it was
already blooming.
What was needed now was a yew.
A columnar yew, fine, straight and tall
as you were.

It must be picked out by me, alone;
transported by me, alone;
dragged from car trunk to yard by me.
Planted by me. Alone.
Its clay-heavy pot lifted over the curb
by me, alone.
The spinal disks popping under the strain,
        immediate.
        Welcomed, even.

How many left behind, bereft, have
cut a finger, slicing tomatoes,
burned a wrist, ironing a shirt,
tripped over a curb, wounding a knee?
The pain of loss, fathoms deep
in the body's fiber, eased only
by a new focus: the pain is *here,*
we tell ourselves; not, as it is,
saturating the entire body,
mind, heart, and the universe.

❧ CLOSURE

I close my eyes,
and imagine yours open.

Tess Gallagher, in "Small Garden Near a Field"

The eyes of the Mayans standing
beside their thatched houses
along the dusty road to Chichén-Itza
have eyes that ever-so-slightly cross,
framing their beautiful aquiline noses.
In infancy, a pendant had been hung
before them to train the eyes inward.
They are in truth beautiful.

We grievers wear a pendant too.
It hangs forever from the middle
of our foreheads. We feel and see it
every waking moment.

Wide-eyed and four, looking up
from his comic book, he'd asked,
"Wonder Woman. Mom,
what did she wonder about?"

A wanderer and wonderer always,
wondering why humans
would cage animals in zoos.
Why some people had no homes;
Why others gave away kittens
to passersby in Harvard Square.

And I, I wonder why anyone
who had lost a loved one
would ever want "closure."

∽ NEVER AGAIN HOMELESS

A phoenix rises as snow melts in rain.
A man edges through an underpass.
Shadows angle from his feet to its ceiling.
He wants to borrow my coat.
For its pockets not its warmth, he says.
We look for turmeric, coriander, cumin.
Egyptian colors, desert colors.
The late autumn-color of liquid heroin
in a saucer. The sounds of sax
angling through a diagonal path
through the diagonal room of the
rest of the restive men without homes.
Some on a visit; some to stay.

He's not here. There is no longer
any here to house him. Only
that small box, and the house of memory:
like that of the poster of pumped bodies
in the weight room in Tucson where
he pumped, not for the pecs or abs,
he said, but "for my kids, to inspire them."
The ones with no homes, abandoned
to the mercy of the state.
With nonchalance he said it. But also
with a pain heard behind the words.

Now, he dances, in slow motion in real time,
in the living room, the LIVING room,
with the wrong genes, but the right heart.
Always and ever, the right heart.

✎ STILL HERE

The banjo. Rehearsal tapes:
hard core, straight-edge.
Vinyl: The Clash; Black 47.
Posters for gigs upcoming:
at The Middle East; the Rat.
Later, tapes catch him
playing Bach, Albeniz.
on the '57 Gibson classic.

EMT badges. Numerous.
Ditto for certificates from rehabs
and NA key chains in various colors.
Thirty days clean. Sixty. Ninety.
John Horton's motorcycle license, issued
to "Johnny Horizon." A mishearing
at the registry? An unshared alter-ego?
a premonition of his own horizon?

School papers: droll, whimsical,
frequently sabotaging assignments
in imaginative ways.
Hand-drawn comic strips featuring
cats, the four-legged kind,
as super heroes: Macavity,
Snicklemoose, Wragg—always "in custody."

Hastily scribbled childhood notes:
"Me and Josh went biking to New Hampshire."
Hand-drawn maps of the planned route,
frequently ending, "Forget it. Too far."
Letters from the Governor, thanking
him for his concern for animals in zoos.

This heart still beating.
This hand, holding this pen.

V

Lady blues singer sings it straight:
The older I get,
The better I know how to spend my time.

ॐ CENTRAL SQUARE SUNDAY, 10 A.M.

The door of the sleek black Buick
opens slowly. Two house-slippered feet
in puffy pink ease their way
down onto the asphalt street.

Passenger-side door opens.
Two more feet slide to the curb.
Four feet swap out slippers
for some fine-looking spiked heels.

Two fine hats, each a symphony
of flowers, feathers, and fruit
are adjusted on heads.

You are fine. Not to be denied.
You are spectacular, elegant,
formidable. Most definitely,
ready this morning
for the procession
down the center aisle
of the AME.

TROIS TABLEAUX, TRÈS VIVANT

1968
A broad back and shoulder,
half inside and half outside
the kitchen window. One leg
in the room; one out.
It'd been that strange rattle
at three a.m. on a windless night
that drew her into the kitchen.

At the first sight of that shoulder
she feels her canines grow longer,
becoming fangs. She becomes
Red Riding Hood, the wolf,
a city-dwelling Mama Grizzly,
a whirlwind of windmilling arms
advancing, shouting imprecations.
The shoulder retracts. Her eyes
follow the shadows following
a man leaping over the back fence,
jumping higher than she thought
any biped could.

1978
The conference is in an upscale
Mid-town Manhattan hotel where
women scholars have gathered
for mutual support.
"There's just no time for
pillow talk with my husband," one
says with an endearing sigh.
Young heads nod in understanding
and sympathy. She listens,
saying nothing.

1988
No window rattles at three a.m. this time.
Just the strong sense that another body
has entered the room. Lifting her head off
the pillow and rising up on an elbow
she finds herself looking into a flashlight
shining in her eyes, blinding her.
She sees only the outline of a tall form,
maybe a leather jacket, maybe not.
Hears no sound but that of two humans
breathing. One considering his options:
            approach? retreat?

The other, deciding to call out, loudly,
some random male name,
as if there were someone in
another room who might respond,
as if two might threaten to outnumber one.

Creaking floorboards tell her
the other body is shifting weight
from foot to foot, pondering a next move,
before turning, retreating slowly
            down the stairs,
                      slipping out the sliding door,

Leaving it, and her, ajar and alone.

WHAT'S IN A NAME

No relation to the Willie Horton,
whose name did far more damage
 to Mike Dukakis' campaign
than whatever might have been
caused by that tank
he was pretending to drive.

Or to the gracious African American
craftsman who laid tile in my house.
Or the equally gracious man
offering the introduction before
the lecture sponsored by the
Africana Studies Department
during Black History Month.
Shaking my hand and his head upon
hearing my name, he did
a quick step back, saying,
"Whoa! Your family
must have owned *my* family!"

Being what used to be called
a "divorcee," I answered:
"It seems for a time,
we were *both* owned by Hortons."

Graciously, he decided to laugh.

❧ BENEFIT PERFORMANCE

The traveling novelists are better
than stand-up comedians.
Their coinage is stories, after all.
Each comes with a stash ready to hand:
heart-warming, droll, themselves often
the butt of their best shticks.
The underwear lost by the hotel laundry.
The hectic multi-city book tour.
Milwaukee tomorrow; the long drive
in the snow to the small East Coast town
where the lone attendee will listen
from her seat amid a sea
of empty folding chairs
in the library basement.

But here, at least, the guests
at the benefit laugh heartily,
admiring the writers' rock-star wit.

But that's only the perspective of
a veteran of podiums—podia?—
at academic conferences. The venue,
always, another sterile mid-town hotel.
Less humor or finery, far more turgid titles,
as *The New York Times* will not fail
to remind its readers on the morrow.
As predictably, those of us on the podia
will shake our heads and marvel,
again this year:
all that booze, and no sex.

✤ LADIES' CHOICE: *MODEH ANI*

Six a.m. Snowy February.
Rise, get ready to shower,
dress, gather notes, graded essays,
and head for the U in time
for the 8:30 class.

Shower knob tells me
pipes are frozen. Head
for basement to see what
can be done.

Blowtorch is there, but no fuel.
Throw on clothes, jump into
old Mazda 626.
Door on driver's side frozen.
Refuses to stay closed.
Book it to Home Depot,
one hand on wheel;
the other holding door shut.

The Modeh Ani will be said anyway:
Gratitude for a new day.
Openness to new possibilities.

Jack will figure out how Sudoku works,
the rabbit will outrun the coyote,
the blow torch will thaw the pipes.
Traffic will be light. Somewhere,
a hurricane veer out to sea.
Somewhere, someone's ache will ease.
At day's end, sleep will be sound;
a new baby born perfect;
a death painless.

❧ IT GOES WITHOUT SAYING

There is no Eleventh Commandment
saying "Thou Shalt Not Eat One Another."
We just, well, *know* that.

Suzanne Langer told us this long ago.
What is presumed to be just "the way things are,"
ingrained in us and in our culture we assume
need be neither articulated nor examined.

But, sometimes, truisms need revisiting.
That Yale handbook, for instance,
distributed to new freshmen in 1968:

"Treat Yale as you would a good woman;
take advantage of her many gifts,
nourish yourself with the fruit of her wisdom,
curse her if you will, but congratulate yourself
in your possession of her."

Written when women still weren't admitted.
It wasn't just Yale; wasn't just "the elites."
"She'll be a fine professor, though a divorcee,"
said the letter in my personnel file.
In that of a well-known and prolific professor,
"Her husband is a distinguished scholar,
and she will be a fine hostess."

What "goes without saying" may just need
to be dusted off, contemplated once more.
Reconsidered before being relegated
finally, to the world of ideas
too frequently held, thought or said,
too infrequently examined.

☙ FOR DON BELTON

Settling into my house for another summer,
you heard me, leaving, call over my shoulder,
"Mi casa, tú casa," and knew I meant it.

Fall marked your leaving, and my return:
me, sweeping up the blizzard of pennies
and crumpled notes you tended to leave
strewn on the floors of every room,
your way of letting me know, I think,
that you'd been comfortable here.

Comfortable we were in our shared loves too.
Jazz, strong coffee, and what Whoopi Goldberg
calls "Negrobelia": that set of boxing black boys
like those in Ralph Ellison's *Invisible Man,* found
in an antique shop, given you for your birthday.
If you were offended, you were kind enough
not to let me know. You must have known
I meant them as support for your own battles.
Now, I see the connection was more freighted
for you: one we could have shared, but didn't.
Maybe you knew I was enmeshed in my own
boxing match, fighting assumptions about what
a high-testosterone but not gay white girl
should want, fight for, or resist. Both of us
suppressing things to keep a roof over our heads,
and soup in the pot.

But I loved you all the same. Loved your neuroses.
Your fear of things like the mercury in tooth fillings.
Neurotic above all about being called neurotic.
Perpetually policing speech, including words
like "black-balled" or "black-listed," whose
connection to racism most couldn't see.

You were, if I could have known it then,
a model to me: policing micro-aggressions,
like the one a former partner endured, his
professor flinging a solicitous arm around him
at the first day's seminar, whispering,
"If you need extra help, let me know."

Your last day here, you'd tried to bleach out the
ink spots you left on the bed coverlet, unwittingly
adding small holes to the ink spots. Now,
I wake every morning to those spots and spaces
covering my body, imagining yours under it,
writing in your journal. The one that led police
to the baby-faced boy-man who took your life
trying to erase his memory of the late-night
encounter you and he had shared.

Both erasures failed: the ink stains and holes
still on the coverlet. The fullness that was you,
still here: the neurotic you, and the brave you,
seeming never to dread or fear the unknown,
living a life as improvised as the jazz we loved.
A black gay man, a writer, bravely
picking up stakes to move wherever
the next teaching gig led, whose trusting
and yearning self proved insufficiently wary.

Every morning still, the eyes of this white girl
settle first on that bright coverlet, reminding me
of the piercings in your body, as beautiful as
the body of St. Sebastian, so often rendered
in paintings as pierced as are the hearts
of all those who remember you still.
After you lost your mother and I my son,
we sang with gusto along with Diana Ross,
 "We are All One Heart."

And so we forever shall be.

✎ BLAME IT ON OUR YOUTH

for Jim Merod

You left. Lit out for the West Coast,
leaving me without a jazz buddy.
Standing solo in the long line at Night Stage,
whose owners couldn't understand
they weren't running a rock club.
This was jazz, I grumbled,
first in line for one of Frank Morgan's
first gigs since exiting the slammer.

Drifting to the stage for sound check
in the still-dark club, he looked up,
caught my ecstatic eyes, and
flashed the Vee I still cherish.

There was no you there, but for consolation,
there was Cecil Taylor later, Gil Evans,
and the Arkestra of Sun Ra, whose young singer's
40s voice could have melted butter, and hearts.

There was Dizzy at the Opera House,
announcing "A Night...A Night..," pausing
until a full house shouted "In Tunisia,"
as if he'd somehow forgotten.
Miles there too. Long after pronouncing ballads
too risky to play. Too easy to slide into
the sentimental, he said. But pacing as usual,
head and trumpet down, that night he succumbed,
spinning a wrenching version
of Cindy Lauper's "Time After Time."

Tom Harrell at the Regatta Bar, speechless
until raising trumpet to lips he became eloquent,
and then some. Sonny Rollins there too,
making his own move from silence to eloquence.

Woody Shaw at the 1369,
mostly blind now—a subway tumble?—
a caring companion leading him gently
to a "stage" doubling as
the path to the bathroom.
George Adams with Cameron Brown
there too, playing their "Song to Sobriety."

Often, the great Alan Dawson on drums,
backbone of so many other great ones,
telling his "lady friend," now my dearest friend,
of the time a sleek car pulled up to the curb
as he mowed his Lexington lawn, its driver
inquiring how much he charged
to do yard work.

Alan, telling her years later as he planted tulips
in that Lexington yard, that he'd not live
to see them come up—
and didn't.

At Bradley's in New York, Junior Mance.
I called you from there once, to tell you
I was listening to Art Farmer.
You passed the word on to Clifford Jordan,
he, saying "Word gets around, man.
Small world."

And so it is. Small, soundful, soulful.

✎ FEBRUARY SUNDAY, FIVE A.M.

Just enough light on the gravel path leading
from the parking lot to the shelter's front door
to catch the glimmer of an empty Coke can
in the moonlight, useful for dropping in
the used needles lying in the frozen grass.
The low glow inside the front door
is welcome this frigid morning.

Pressing the button alerts staff I'm here.
Stepping inside, feeling—or imagining—
the guests' breaths rising and falling in unison
as they sleep on rows of cots in the big room.
Soft sounds of a radio turned low at the
front desk offer Otis Redding, keeping
Calvin and Lita awake to the end
of their overnight shift.

Wheeling carts into the laundry room,
stuffing a line of industrial-size washers
with sheets and a bit of soap before heading
to the kitchen, grateful Calvin's already
broken open the twelve dozen eggs,
hoping he won't suffer sore thumbs all day;
knowing too well breaking that many eggs hurts.

Hoping to find a canned ham or two
in the walk-in to dice into the scrambled eggs.
Hoping the van picking up the street sleepers
during the night came back with enough
day-old muffins and bagels. Hoping they've
not been tumbled together in the trash bag
so the muffins' icing will need to be scraped
off the bagels: hoping they're not poppy seed,
messing up drug tests some guests will take.

Showered and dressed, guests line up
at seven, each one fortified with enough
hot coffee to get them through another
day stemming on the streets, or maybe
just to find some way to pass the long hours
until the shelter doors open again at four.
There's an armrest at the center of
the new benches the city's just put in.
Curling up on one to keep out the cold
isn't possible any more.

Still, they line up quietly, resigned to what
the day will or won't bring, greeting me
with warmth and whimsy. I am "Miss Ohio,"
and sometimes "Goldilocks," while they are,
each of them, who they are: lawyers,
veterans, women and men. Ordinary people
showing extraordinary tenderness
to one another: making sure Eddie
in the wheelchair gets his tea hot,
with two sugars and a straw; teaching
Bobby how to hook the straps on his
yellow rain gear before he heads out;
taking care that the last blueberry muffin
gets saved for Marty, while I,
standing at the window serving up ham and eggs,
am the ornery vegan, asking each one, sweetly,
"Would you like some animal products
        this morning?"

They, chuckling, and I, already missing
        each one of them:
                then, and still.

VI

Here no elsewhere
underwrites my existence.

Philip Larkin, in
"The Importance of Elsewhere"

ᔐ FINDING HOME

Now, home is where the hart is.
And the fox, the coyote, snapping turtle,
seal, shark, whale, whimbrel and willet.

Hang a right at the weedy lot
anchored by a weathered
upturned dory.

After a quick left, the asphalt drops away,
replaced by a sandy, rutted
excuse for a road.
You can go no farther,
nor do you want to.

A cottage of wash-ashore boards
sits there, jerry-built; jerry-renovated.
By whom can't be known.
Stories tend to grow here,
sticking like barnacles to people
and the places they live in,
both getting more fantastical with time.
"Why, that cottage washed ashore whole
 after a storm years ago!"
said the man who'd owned it long ago.
All that's certain are the woods:
woods in front; woods behind.

All that's certain is what's visible.
Storm windows, but no windows;
a porch passing for a living room.

Call it a shotgun shack if you want.
I'll not care. I'm home.

❧ VEGANOMICS

Go to the meat market of a Saturday night
and see the crowds of live bipeds staring up
at the long rows of dead quadrupeds. Does not
that sight take a tooth out of the cannibal's jaw?
Who is not a cannibal.

> In the "Whale as a Dish"
> chapter of *Moby Dick*

So mused Melville's Ishmael.
Dickens' Bumble must've thought so too,
grumbling that Oliver Twist's outbursts
were caused by "Meat! Meat, ma'am!"

But upon the arrival of every new baby,
Dickens' celebratory dinner invitations sent
to friends frequently announced that
the spit would begin to turn at seven,
never failing to point out that
he'd be spearing the roast, not the baby.

Veganomical ambivalence is hardly unusual.
Who could help but dream, for instance, of
those knee-high fringed moccasin boots.
The ones with the soft, rounded soles
for sale in that catalogue coming from
the Southwestern Indians.

With those, the smidgen of Indian in me
might walk the trails in the woods and dunes
the first residents here had trod, and feel
a bit less a trespasser treading sacred ground.

If only it were possible to wear those boots
without thinking about the deer sacrificed
so I could feel that softness, that sexy.

But oh, dear Southwestern Indians,
send me instead that bag of bean soup mix;
that fetching hemp bag of pistachios;
that beautiful mesh bag of soaps
redolent with the smells of
   piñon pine,
     lemon verbena,
       prickly pear.

They'll be sensory reminders of
New Mexico's mountains and
Arizona's sand and red rock.

Almost as good as those sexy boots.

   Almost.

℘ LANGUAGE ACQUISITION II

> Of all the love bonds, the strongest...lay
> between a father and his daughter-baby. This
> was recognized in Cape family life, and
> gradually the goodmen came to give it a name.
> The daughter-baby was the father's tortience.

> Elizabeth Reynard, in *The Narrow Land.*

The columnist writing for a local paper long ago
reveled in describing how much she enjoyed throwing
"summer sweets" into a saucepan to be "chunked" with
water and sugar; loved regaling her readers with her
enthusiasm for things like the "denatured wood pussy"
she'd just seen at the fair.

In old books about this old arm flexing into the sea,
wonderful words: "old luggers"—boats—harvesting
oysters, while millers were known as "dry-land
sailors," because a windmill required old sailors,
adept at keeping the sails of windmills as right
to the wind as those on the boats they used to sail.

A "pickle," a small plot of land connected by a
hedgerow; a "tombolo," a sand or gravel bar
connecting an island with the mainland,
or with another island, as one loner might become
friends with another, one supposes.

Would that such colorful words could return:
Like the description of Mary Walley, the minister's
daughter, "eyable, knowful, and yonderly of heart."

Who wouldn't want to be so clearly seen,
so beautifully described. Say it again:
"eyable, knowful, and yonderly of heart."

᧡ THE CAPE COMPLAINER

How could you not love this spit of land?
Be bothered in the night by the coyote, whose
howls had the wheeze of a smoker with
a two-pack a day habit? How not be
mesmerized by the owl's midnight hoots?
Not love walking the weaving path beside
dune grass, sea lavender, or goldenrod
rustling in the fall winds?

Instead, frowns, at shrink-wrapped boats
waiting for summer in side yards.
In flags flapping in ocean breezes
beside front doors of shake-shingled half-Capes
you saw right-wing leanings, where I see
affectionate nods to simpler times.

Driving roads rife with echoes of Micah Rafe
and spirits of other First Light people,
you rued the names our roads carry:
Uncle Venie's Road; Jan's Path; Clifford's Way.
Why begrudge Aunt Katie her Pond?
The Sachems at least their claim to their names?

No point in recounting to you the tale
of old Granny Squannit, who legend tells us
had "the otherness of woman" about her.
Or of the giant Meloof, here even before
glaciers carved out the kettle ponds, his arms
so long he could touch Provincetown with one hand
and Orleans with the other, his fishing pole
made of a two-hundred foot pine.
Or old giant Maushop, still veiling our roads
in magical fog each time he takes a long stride
over the waters of Nantucket Sound,
puffing on his giant pipe.

↬ JOE THE BEAGLE

The meandering river
lifts the bays of the lost beagle,
carrying them over the roofs
of summer homes shuttered for the winter.
Ever quieter and further off, his bays
drift over the roofs of Trinity Cove,
of Old Mill Point, hovering
before sliding over the rain-darkened
pavement of Lower County Road,
carless at 3 a.m.

It had been dusk, and his people
not yet home. No electric fence
could shock or stop him.
He needed to rescue them.
To guide them home.

But his Beagle system is all outward bound.
Fine for tracking; useless for back-tracking.
His snout has no GPS, so in the
deepening darkness he finds himself
lost, muddied, exhausted, scratched and bruised.

So are his people. After driving slowly
up and down the empty streets, they now
find themselves walking through back yards
abandoned for the season.

In their rain slickers they wave flashlights,
calling out his name: "Joe! Joe!"
Blocks away, always blocks away,
his bays keep drifting over the water:
"Here! I'm over here...."

❧ JOEY

If cats still rode the rails,
you'd be one of 'em. You
could've been the model
for those curled cats 'thirties
hard times hoboes chalked
on sidewalks to let other cats know
a kind woman who might
give them some grub
lived nearby.

Just how many kind ladies
do *you* visit, and what whim
sends you to a particular back door
with that anticipating look
on any particular day?

Just in the neighborhood
and thought you'd stop by?
Are particularly fond of the
brand of food offered there?

May I some day come to know
the answer to those questions,
and you, to feel safe enough
to allow and enjoy a scratch
behind the ears: to learn that
an under-the-chin rub is at least
as satisfying as a can of Fancy Feast
gulped between one of your random
travels through one of your random routes
through the world.

OCTOBER, WEST DENNIS BEACH

> Yes, as everyone knows, meditation
> and water are wedded forever.
>
> Herman Melville, in *Moby Dick*

Her long dark hair is as wind-whipped as the paper
she clutches and reads from for a long, long time.
When she finishes, the half-moon of
young bodies drifts to the shoreline
as if tied together by heart-strings.
Once there, one kneels,
opens and empties the small box
into the waves. Its content becomes,
for just one moment,
a swirl of dust and ash.

A short ways away, an unsteady toddler squeals,
tumbles into the soft sand, ignoring
her father's upward-pointing finger
and excited cry: 'kite!" "kite!"

The bony finger of the mother whose wheelchair
a daughter has wheeled closer to the
water's edge points outward
to soaring herring gulls
and a paraglider's cambering sails,
her desiccated chuckle
drifting over the waves
like the ashes on the Ganges
young boys swim among.

❧ APRIL: APERÇUS ASKEW

Headed across the road for a
quick mailbox trek
in early fog, movement's
caught aslant at the
eye's outermost edge.

At theirs too, prompting
their swift sideways glide
back into the woods
after a liminal pause
a safe ways away and
a glance over the haunch
at the two-legged thing that is me.

Me, glancing out of eye corner too,
catching glimpse of coyote, fox, or deer.

Later, reading on the window seat
at window's ledge on a windy day,
my vision's edge catches movement:

a blowing leaf or hopping bird;
me, craning to see which.

✍ MIDDEN IN THE FRONT YARD

Digging post holes for the split rail fence,
it was middens that kept turning up
as the sandy soil was being turned over.
Neatly piled shells, left behind
by the earliest clammers. I pause, pay homage,
apologize, and mourn for each one, each
a member of one of the thirty tribes
living here, along the Herring River,
migrating overland with the seasons between
Nantucket and what is now called Cape Cod:
part of the 15,000 and maybe even 45,000
People of the First Light who lived, worked,
raised food and family here and nearby.

In Dennis, Nobscussets.
      In Yarmouth, Hockanoms.
           In Falmouth, Succonesitts.
In Sandwich, Manomets.
      In Barnstable and Yarmouth,
           Mattakees and Cummaquids.
In Chatham, Monomoyicks.
      In Eastham and Orleans, Nausets.
         In Truro, Pamets.
 In Rhode Island, Narragansetts, Pocasets,
      Nemaskets, Mohegans, Pokanoket.

Each tribe led by a great sachem:
      Aspinet, Massasoit, Iyannough,
      Canonicus, Caubitant,
      Uncas, Wo'ipeguand among them.

Names often mangled in books,
the ears of English speakers unused
to the softer sounds of Wôpanâak speech.

It's said First Peoples often sang
themselves to sleep at night.
Invited to overnight with
Winslow and other early settlers,
their quiet singing often left their
hosts waking grouchy from lack of sleep.

Samuel de Champlain, an even
earlier visitor, wrote of the neat
appearance of Nauset girls. "But,"
writes a later, editorializing historian,
"sailors are not always discriminating
in matters of feminine beauty. It was
a long time since Champlain had seen
any women, and he doubtless looked
upon them with a tolerant eye."

"The men wore no clothes to speak of,"
reports another, "until cold weather
forced them into a single lower garment
of deerskin serving as both trousers
and stockings, another deerskin worn
loosely over the upper part of the body."

Mourt's Relation is filled with
descriptions of those bodies.
"Comely," they're called;
"well-formed, adorned with
feathers and beads, near naked."

It could be this fascination—
call it attraction, as it surely was—
is why they just had to be killed.
Reduced by at least two-thirds
by disease, plague, and war.

A story so old, it's new.

∾ TRASH TALK

The bag in the trunk stunk.
It was those toadstools tossed in
with the grass clippings and weeds,
now festering in the hot car.

All made worse by the kitchen trash
that's left fishy cat food scraps
sticking to the Velcro brace covering
the fractured wrist. The one I just used
to wave an apology on my way to the dump.

The one aimed at the driver who'd yelled
out his car window an ironic "Thank you!!"
when I failed to let him make that left turn
against traffic. An oldtimer, washashore
courtesy I'd just failed to honor.

Waving my brace out the window
had been my attempt to let him know
I didn't let him go ahead because
it hurt too much to downshift my old
standard transmission auto. Probably
he thought I was giving him the finger.

Back home, smarting from the insult
and the pain turning the key in the door causes,
changing clothes I notice the Velcro
on the brace is catching on the material
of my new shirt, leaving sprigs of
torn thread sprouting and curling
as I struggle one-handed to tuck shirt into shorts.

Heading for a scrap of paper
to record this summer moment,
I can find no pen.

✌ RIGHTEOUS BEACHWALKER

Another plastic bag on the shore
needing to be scooped up, along with
the remnants of deflated helium balloons,
all silvery plastic and ribbon strings.
Released in celebration, now far too tempting
to seabirds and fish who catch sight
of that glitter, mistake it for the silvery scales
of edible creatures, and eat it,
messing up their insides,
sometimes unto death.

Visions of pictures in wildlife magazines
showing autopsies of dead bird innards
fill my mind as I stride to scoop it up
before it does harm. But drawing nearer
I see what the herring gull has been
dragging through the sand with
such purpose. It's no balloon.
No plastic bag.

It's the head and spine of a fine big striper
a fisherman has gutted and filleted.
Remains thrown overboard, where
they've ended, floating in my sea of negativity,
bobbing beside my righteous indignation,
slowly transforming now
into a small glimmer of hope
in a despairing age.

Or would be, if I could cease worrying
about fish bones lodging in
that minister gull's throat,
wondering if, and then hoping,
there might be a Saint Valentine
for gulls.

✎ BEAUTIFUL STRANGERS

Mid-summer, mid-Cape, mid-day.
Janeo sits sorting photos she intends
to put into albums, until she runs out
of time or interest, and piles them all
back into the shoe boxes again.

A languid watcher, I sit and muse until
catching a glimpse of a particular photo,
"Who's that?" explodes from my mouth.
She slides the photo in question across
the sunny picnic table. I see the photo
is of her parents, lounging at the beach
in their sexy prime, cigarettes dangling
from their lips.

It's a sweet photo. But studying it,
I think of the photos we all have:
of the high school graduations; of family
unwrapping gifts under the Christmas tree.
I think of how banal most of our photos are.

Until my eyes catch in the background
of that photo of her parents the image
of a stunning young hunk of a boy-man,
a pack of Chesterfields rolled up tight
in the sleeve of his muscle shirt.

When I ask her "Who is *that*?
she says "I have no idea!"
But there he is. Captured. A beautiful
James Dean, doing what a James Dean does:
 just ambling on by.

But now *I'm* the one who is captured.
Does this James Dean hunk have any idea
his image has been preserved in *this* shoebox,
on this patio? Is being savored this sunny
Cape Cod day, while somewhere
just at this moment and these many years later
his bored wife is gazing at her snoozing husband
in his Barcalounger, a half-read
newspaper draped over his knees?

And then I wonder: in how many strangers'
photo shoeboxes have *I* been caught,
having wandered into shooting range
as a vacationing family snapped selfies
during its day at Nauset Beach.

And if so, oh, please tell me it was
while I still wore a bikini. Or at least
was not wearing those sunglasses.
The ones that always sat askew on my nose.

And promise me, please, that fifty years
hence, as someone's grandchildren
peruse photos of their own family
at Nauset beach, they'll not be squinting
at my face and form in the background,
wondering, "Could that be great aunt Sarah?"
Or asking, "Who is that weird lady
standing behind Savannah and Jaydan
in those goofy sunglasses?"

ॐ DYSLEXIC ON THE WHALE WATCH

"Finback at four o'clock!"
the excited naturalist announces.
I shift eyes and feet. Take a tentative step
to the right, to the left: right; left again.

Where is four o'clock anyway?
Starboard, as in to the right?
But is that looking toward the *front*
of the boat—that would be forward,
toward the bow. Stem to stern
means front to back, but which
is "stem," and which "stern" here?

Port would be Left, stern directly Aft.
Alee, away from wind; windward, toward.
These things make sense to me, but only
because they involve words, not space.

Meanwhile, my brow furrows,
as fluke of minke, right, or finback
slides back into the depths. Unseen.

Our brains include place cells,
grid cells, and head-direction cells
so we can orient ourselves.
I know this. I read this.

But facing the map at trail's head
in hiking boots and lugging backpack
a day later, this dyslexic hiker sighs.
You see my problem here.

ASSISTED LOVING

Back in Ohio, weary of the sauerkraut
served too often at lunch at the facility
where she now lives—
what symphony of lacked sympathy
inspired such a diet to now-sedentary
folks is a mystery worth pondering—
Mom calls to confess a great hunger
for a nice acorn squash.
Baked.

Rushing to the market, her daughter
eight hundred miles away
selects the biggest squash in the pile,
mails it overnight express,
throwing in a nice mellow red
to go with it.

The thank you call the next day
includes a sigh: no corkscrew
can be found.

That item is sent overnight express too,
wrapped in a note saying,
"Because it was an emergency."

A phrase to be repeated and enjoyed
all the way to the end of her life.

ॐ GIRL AT THE REST STOP

Somewhere between
the eastern and western terminus
of the Pennsylvania turnpike,
at one of its older rest stops,
the smell of frying fatty meat hovers
thick in the air, clinging
to the clothes of wayfarers
stopping there.

There seems to be only one
place at this auto oasis where
a fruit smoothie might be
found and downed
before hitting the road again.

Threading the space between
Formica tables and plastic chairs
in search of that smoothie,
I spy a twelve-year old girl
doing a Virabhadrasana One.
As ungraceful a Warrior One
as most we do are. But she *is*
another oasis here.
Whether she's stretching
or just showing off, no matter.
Would she have read my joining her
as support, or intrusion into
her private performance?
Should I have asked?

∿ THE TEACHER TAUGHT

For Jack Fraser

You were the first after the hospice training.
Me, tiptoeing in trepidation to the threshold
of your nursing home room to ask if
you might like a bit of company.
Music before conversation, I'd thought.
Could I rip a few CDs of your favorites,
not speaking to the obvious: that they might
help you pass the time between this day,
and however many you might have left.

Soon we were friends: sitting side by side,
you in your wheelchair, both of us gazing
out the wide window at the end of the hall
at the woods beyond, our feet resting on the
window ledge while you, a lanky former runner,
pointed a bony finger to show me the path
you'd be taking if you could still run.
You never complained. Not once.

When I'd asked what music you liked,
no particular answer was expected;
for certain not the one you gave: "the Beatles."
So Beatles it was for months—until the day
I arrived, took a good close look
at your ravaged face and form, and saw
that Maxwell Silver Hammer
just wasn't going to do it anymore.

So it was the sweet voices of Irish women
singing in Irish that ushered you out;
your last labored, whispered words to me,
"The Irish are a spiritual people." As were you.

❧ ESTATE SALE TREASURES

The diplomats had spent distinguished lifetimes
in the foreign service, assigned to, living in,
and growing to love the countries and cultures
they served around the globe.

In the end, it all came down to an estate sale.
An absolute sale, it's called, and it surely was that:
the accumulated treasures of a lifetime
displayed— splayed out—it seemed to me
on long tables in their basement.

Visited by Sunday morning browsers,
aimless or curious. By bargain seekers,
picking up and setting down the Mexican dolls,
the coffee mug from Kuwait; the cowhide purse
crafted in Africa. Some of it genuine folk art,
and some of it touristy kitsch, resting alongside
books on birding and building, anthologies of
Shakespeare plays, photos of South African towns,
next to personal family photos like the one
of the wife on camel back in Egypt.

Upstairs, forgotten furs hanging in closets.
Cupboards bursting with more treasures
amassed over fifty years
by two vital lives, now gone.

Piece by piece picked up, studied, and then
put back down, as will be so much
of our own life, at its end.

Each of us will do our own housekeeping
on schedule: shedding and shucking,
as we will, and must.

VII

✑ IMAGO AMIGOS

Imago: An insect in its final,
sexually mature, typically winged
state. Or, an idealized version of
another, or the self.
Plural: *imagoes* or *imagines*.

Merriam Webster's Dictionary

Imagines imagined.
Or, maybe, that dragonfly,
winged: *alar,* four squares
on the crossword grid,
seven down.
Seven decades too.
Few to go,
friends.

ɔ LATE-LIFE BLOOMING

My mother was a beautiful woman, physically,
and as she got older, spiritually....
The older she got, the more beautiful
the attitude and the closer we got
to each other.

> Miles Davis, in *Miles: The*
> *Autobiography*

Threshold. A word that began as a way to describe the
place where wheat is threshed: separated from chaff.
The kind of separation that might mark, say,
the end of one way of looking over a long life,
       and another.

At least when you married in 1939,
the mangle was no longer in use.
But the wringer washer was.
You almost became a cliché one day.
Were almost put through the wringer. I watched
as your arm was being swept inexorably
toward the washer's roller, your fingers
caught as you were pushing the dripping pieces
of clothes close—too close—
to that moving wringer.

Terrified, I was, and too young to know how to help.
Now I think you must have felt that way even
when the wringer washer was nowhere near.

And who wouldn't? Who wouldn't sniffle a bit
from time to time, seeing her dreams of being
a lady buried beneath those piles of laundry,
or being hung out to dry.

The sniffles and sighs were replaced over time.
The Oxydol, Lava Soap, perfection salads,
Westinghouse and Ipana all still present,
but now there was music on the radio—Paul Whiting,
Glenn Miller, Guy Lombardo, Mantovani,
Eddy Duchin—and the soaps.

After the vacuum was put away for the day,
your children coming home from school
often found you with one leg draped
leisurely over the arm of the rocker
as you watched the small TV, munching
liberally-buttered popcorn
from your favorite bowl.

You never asked whether we wanted any.
And why should you?
You'd never asked us, not even once,
like the Little Red Hen, "Who will help me...?
"Not I," was always the answer.

I see now that we were the "Not I" children.
Too dense to take the hint, if it was one.
Never helping with the laundry, the cleaning.
Maybe you were teaching us
the importance of self-reliance—
or of the value of denial. Or both.

Whichever it was, in the end
you came to full bloom.
Found your voice. A strong one.
As Iraq was being invaded,
hissing between your teeth in fury,
 "I'll kill W myself! I'm old.
They'll never know I was the one that did it!"

✑ THE SWIMMER

For Mary Lou Holland

We're the wrong size, Loren Eiseley mused.
 Too small to see galaxies,
 but too large to see with our eyes
 the tiny world of atoms, molecules, cells.

Kafka mused in one of his Paradoxes
that humans are fettered to earth by a chain
long enough to roam the earth,
but tethered at the same time
by a heavenly chain.
If we try to roam the earth, the
heavenly collar throttles us.
If we strain to reach heaven,
the earthly one does the same.

So there you are, dearest friend.
You've sat with so many
heading to the other side,
and now find yourself
well past eighty,
hovering between realms.

What can I say to you while you hover?
That loving all your life swimming in the ocean,
suspended between two realms,
you've already spent a lifetime
both of, and not of, earth?

For now, you tread. Walk the earth,
while in a way treading water too:
waiting to leave, wondering
how long to stay;
how much more pain to endure.

Having suffered our share of losses
at least brings a sort of wisdom.
You and I know this.
"Remember the good times,"
those who've not yet known loss
advise, not yet having experienced
the wisdom in Louise Glück's
"The Burning Heart": that
"No sadness is greater than
in misery to rehearse memories
        of joy."

Cavalier counselors full of advice
like this are all wrong.
They've never lost a child,
as we have.

But wrong, too, were our lost loved ones:
failing to outlive their beloved dogs,
or us. Having had a body hosting
all the elements that make up a star,
how could they dare leave us,
long before we think their star
should have burned out?

∾ NO FOOTPRINTS

Whatever you choose to claim
of me is always yours;
nothing is truly mine
except my name. I only
borrowed this dust.

Stanley Kunitz, in "Passing Through—
on my seventy-ninth birthday"

For years, our mother yanked the cord from
the wall socket across the room after vacuuming,
wanting to leave no footprints.
This regularly wrecked the cord, irritating just slightly
her patient husband, responsible for the repair.

Now I see leaving no footprints is not a bad idea.
Not even in the soon-enough-to-be vacated life.
Not in the dust of Cambridge's Common our feet
packed down during protests as Vietnam raged.

Not those left in the dusty streets of Juarez,
nor the sandy ones of El Paso. Nor in Hawaii's
mountain trails slick with the mush of fallen guavas
on the paths leading to its magical waterfalls.

Poets might hope the best of their work
will be encountered and read in winter,
when time is slowed, darkness comes early
and lasts long, and lines slowly absorbed
while roads remain slushy as memory,
shadows long, days short,
and snowy footprints easily erased
by weather, tides, rain, snow,
wind-blown sands, or time itself.

∽ POEM FOR A YOGA NOMAD

for Michele

They say there are 108 names for god.
One of them must be no-god.
There are 4,000 yoga poses, some say,
all but one hundred of which
we will never master.

"Stretch a little deeper," you say, and we do,
recognizing that the stretching
that must be done is partly
a stretching towards acceptance.
Head to knee perfection
may never happen.
A perfect wheel will not occur.
But acceptance of our place on
the wheel of life will.

The tissue-thin stone full of tiny holes
picked up on the shore today
is rock, on its way to becoming sand.

No force or will of its own, but the tides
will push the tiny particles it is shedding
from this shore to a farther one.
And yes we, too, will go a little deeper
and a little farther—in time.

℘ RECTIFYING THE NAMES

Asked what he would do if given a land
to govern, Confucius said he would
rectify the names. Not a bad idea.

"Heart rendering," my neighbor says,
a revision far better than the original.
My father's late-life vocabulary was laced
with such linguistic improvements, just as
his treatment of his children's illnesses
he was convinced could be cured by
OTC meds he was sure could
out-perform any doctor's prescription.
Ergophine, Mentholypsis. Alum chunks,
mini icebergs, miraculously curing canker sores—
but only if held inside the lip until tears came.

At his end, his words didn't fall away.
It's just that better ones kept arriving.
Fishing now required not night-crawlers,
but "moonshiners." Richard's last words,
to me were an elegant three: "Rich in Heaven,"
capping a lifetime of deft name-giving: to
his brother Snubby; to Tootie and his wife Babe;
to cousins Poke and Diddy.

His children were used to this, though
they did wonder about neighborhood nemesis
Butchie. Was a child *christened* Butchie,
or just became one by reputation?

Just thinking about him gives me goosebumples.

↬ WEEDING

Auch kleine dinge können uns entzucken.
[Small things can also delight us.]
Franz Schubert

It's spindly and pallidly chartreuse,
though its roots had been promising as a poem.
Neither produced the expected profusion.
No astillbe, artemesia, anemone, bee balm,
bleeding heart, coreopsis, dianthus, epimideum,
heliotrope, down to zinnia, of course.

The weeding is best done on your knees.
The poem about your old lover,
some childhood embarrassment:
best to crop it, lop it, pull it out
leaf, branch, and root.

The poetry "process" is something
more like the unexpected rudbeckia
that springs up in Spring from seeds
shat from a passing bird.

The rest—not tied with ribbons like
Emily's poems—might best end
in the recycling truck, sifting down
to the bottom to meet there
the stacks of notes on the habits of bees,
turtle migrations, twenty-minute meal recipes,
and home remedies for poison ivy.

Maybe best to forget about things
recollected in tranquility.
Just weed, lop, and crop.

⚘ UPENDED LIVES

An hour's walk along the beach reveals receding tide
has deposited seven hundred and forty-three upended
shells of horseshoe crabs in the sand.
On just this one foggy Sunday morning.

Seven hundred and forty-three ancient arthropods:
living fossils who've survived for four hundred million
years on this planet, now threatened with extinction.

Their blood—called hemocyanin for its blue hue—
is used in the treatment of some ailing humans,
and who could argue with that.
"Harvesting," it's called. After the "harvesting,"
each "donor" is returned to the sea.
But for every five hundred thousand who "donate,"
a hundred fifty thousand don't survive.

My toe turns over each upturned shell to see which
have just shucked a shell they've outgrown.
But if the pedipalps—legs—are still there,
you can count that one among the hapless "donors."

There is no longer a Paradise, of course, even here.
And how many of us are guilty of upending
something or someone? A marriage, a life or lives,
children, someone's hopes, a job: the list could go on.

I Would Have Saved Them if I Could,
Leonard Michaels titled a novel.
I, too, have always wanted to save
somebody or something: those arthropods,
younger siblings, an old cat, a young seal, a son,
other bereft and bereaved parents;
the addicted, homeless and struggling.

And the innocent animals of course,
like that intelligent pig
whose story was recounted
in the local paper.

He, greeting his farmer each morning
with eager eyes, following him
around the barnyard, thinking himself
companion and friend, unaware his destiny
was to be the ham in someone's sandwich,
until the farmer just couldn't
surrender him up for the slaughter.

A rare triumph for pig and man
in a world where every gift of Nature,
every tall old scrub pine
or ancient arthropod
is seen too often only as a "resource"
to be monetized:
a "growth" opportunity
in one economy,
while shriveling the spirit
and shrinking the soul
in another.

❧ THE BLOOD OF MURDERED TREES

There it was again. The same feeling felt stumbling
upon the body of that young seal, still with downy fur,
lying dead in the sand. Or looking into the sad eyes
of the old cat languishing in the communal cage
at the shelter, surrounded by gamboling kittens,
now snoozing in the sun on my window seat.
Her eyes had held the same look seen in the eyes
of people without homes at that other shelter:
equal parts need, and chagrin at needing.

This time it wasn't a look, or the sound of chainsaws.
It was the smell of the sap, their blood,
driving me from my house across the road
from where a house will be jammed between
street and swale, making homeless the great horned
owl, the coyote, the box turtle who lumbers
each year across the road to lay her eggs.
All being sacrificed to a bipedal flipper.

Only a flight to the shore would soothe:
to watch cormorants on the jetty pulsing
their out-stretched wings to dry,
in full crane pose.

To see if today the wrack harbors a small
translucent body with no organs inside:
the palest of pinks, stitched together only
with a fine pink thread down its center.
It seems to sit atop a cerulean shell.
But that shell turns out to be soft. It houses
the tentacles of the Portuguese man 'o war.
Beauty and pain in one package.

Sometimes a sting waits in the warmest of waters.

✌ STILL, AND YET: SMOOTH SAILING

No Robert Moses decided in the 'forties
that the new highway needed to slice through
the middle of my neighborhood, cutting me off
from friends and family a block away.
Or from any job I needed to get to.
No toxic waste site was located nearby.
No lead-laden water ran through the pipes.

No George Wallace blocked my way
when I arrived to enroll in the local college.

No suspicion flickered on the face
of the security person following me
when I told him I'd forgotten to remove a tag
from the jacket bought for my three year old.

No money for a car during the struggling years,
but no worries about getting to work.
Public transit was available and nearby.

No ticket was issued by the State-y when
I absent-mindedly glided through a stop sign.
Only a warning, a smile, and a warm wave instead.

Only one mortgage officer at one bank
said "we don't go in there" when I applied
to purchase that triple decker
in a black neighborhood.

Only one addict shooting up escaped arrest
during the raid on the shooting gallery,
the police telling my son,
"go on home, college boy."

This Little Red Hen is white. She had help aplenty.

THE THINGS WE CARRY: ANCESTORS, PACKING

> The pulling of a trigger or the touching
> of an arm can be understood only through
> the intersection of neuron construction, brain
> chemistry, evolution, childhood environment,
> and societal structure.
>
> Robert Sapolsky, in *Behave: The Biology*
> *of Humans at our Best and Worst.*

Suitcases. Boxes. Baby carriage.
Sewing machine. Tools.
Beside the front door,
stacked flail, sickle, and scythe.
Willem and pretty Elizabetha, you are
one more German immigrant family
leaving one more small Michigan farm.
The sepia photo tells your story.

Nine children, three already lost.
You'll not move as far as your son Charles
and his Rose, soon enough packing
their things and their babies too,
five soon swelling into twelve.
Bay City to Ohio,
Roseanna baying silently
then, and for all her life.

Lewis and Clara, did you think
you could run your Ohio farm alone?
Lewis, how did you come to work
in that factory instead, and at sixty-five?
What exactly did you do there?
Run machinery, or just sweep shavings?

And how did you manage to accrue six mortgages,
losing even your small house?
Was it bad habits, or just bad luck?

Frank and 'Liza, did you keep glancing
over your shoulders as your tractor rumbled
north and then west, from Ohio to Owosso
during the hungry '30s, checking to see
whether the revenue man
was in hot pursuit?

Did you worry for your nine children
following along behind? Did you know
they'd not be farmers anymore?
Welders, seamstresses, domestics instead?

When you left Quebec for Bay City
with two babies in tow, Edward and Alivine,
was your English even passing fair?
Did you choose Bay City
for its French-speaking Churches?

Once settled, Edward, did your suitcase
sit, always packed, by the door?
Canada to Michigan, Michigan to Canada,
back and forth over the border,
following lumberjack seasons,
and maybe wild lumberjack ways?

What of my own baggage
came from each of you?
Wanderlust? The stiff upper lip?
A capacity to make do, to do wrong,
to always look over my shoulder
to see what had been left behind?

ℒ YUP'IK TEARS

> I think that those who made so many things
> ought to be masters of everything.
> And those who make bread ought to eat!
>
> Pablo Neruda, from "El Pleno"

For twenty years Peter Freuchen lived in
northernmost Eastern Canada, married to
Navarana. They had two children.
Famous Book of the Eskimos, a collection
of his essays, became a best-seller in 1957.
In one, he describes how women scratched
in the frozen ice through the long winters'
endless darkness, looking for heather
to burn for their cooking fires.
With no daylight, they did it by feel.
Gloves couldn't be used. They were left
with hands dark brown, hard as wood,
and long nails, curved,
　　　like the talons of eagles.

They did their cooking in tiny huts away
from the family igloo, not wanting
to smoke up the abode of the man of the house.
Lying flat in there—the ceiling was low—
they blew on the fires made with that heather.
Its sparks singed their faces, its smoke
tearing their eyes, turning the whites red.
Their icy tears carved raw rivulets down their cheeks.
　　　Those rivulets never healed.

A great-great grandmother went blind from
tending the fire while baking bread, I was told.
I have no name: only gratitude, grief, these words,
　　　and her Yup'ik blood in my veins.

✎ SCRUB PINES

I

They wind-dance with limbs akimbo
like Steve Martin in "The Jerk," until
their limbs dry out like ours as we bend
to pick them up after they've snapped
in a storm. We hope our own won't.

But they endure, mostly, as we do:
by bending into the wind as we walk
the blustering beach, unlike the
rigidly upright young, slim, pliable
and newly planted, prone too easily
to break in stormy times.

II

There's dead center, and the dead bolt.
You're either dead right, or dead wrong.
Deep asleep, you're dead to the world.

III

Sooner or later, we all end as dead fall:
fallen trees, available for burning,
to keep the living warm.

IV

As for me, I only borrowed this fuel.
Take it, burn it: the old tree branches,
these pages, these stories, we are
each and all,

altogether bio-degradeable.

⤳ LAST CONFESSION

> A book must be the ax for
> the frozen sea within us.
>
> Franz Kafka, Letter to Oskar
> Pollak, January 27, 1904.

Checking the atlas, looking for the location of
that little Italian town you've always longed to visit,
you often find it's hidden in the seam of the atlas.

Workers in binderies call that the gutter:
the space at the center of a book
where the pages are stitched together.
The last words of a too-long line of a poem, say,
risk dropping off there: invisible, unreadable.

Like the chapters and stages of a life
hidden in the seams and joins of the repairs
made to the wood in the old house of memory.
The ones that might best be left unexposed,
except by ones curious or naive enough
to avoid the gutter, or daring enough to expose
the fault lines between who and what we were,
who we still are, and who we are no longer.

The woman on the cover here is sanding a door.
She'll sand it to a fine, smooth surface,
then give it multiple coats of high-gloss varnish.
Exactly as her father had done making her desk
fifty years and more ago.
It'll become the desk she'll write on.

She sees now that her back in that photo
looks like *his* back as she watched him dig,

from shift's end until darkness fell,
shovelful by clay-heavy shovelful,
a basement under their small house:

She'll also turn out to be the Little Red Hen,
never asking for or knowing how to accept
any help or suggestions offered.
She'll repair the leak, paint the shingles,
grade the papers, lug the yew tree
of mourning to the yard and plant it. Alone.

She'll continue to love swings: porch swings,
backyard swings; swing dancing in Tucson;
the swing of bat meeting ball, but unwilling
to be any other kind of swinger,
losing a life and a family with a sadness
still present, still vivid.

Naiveté is always either willed arrogance
or ignorance: either believing the wrong thing
can be easily fixed, or if not, just ignored—
Freud was right at least about that—
and loss and grief hammered into acceptance,
with enough time, effort, and a dollop
of the old stiff upper lip.

But those things are as elusive as the route to
that small Italian town hiding in the atlas gutter, or
in the binding of the pages you hold in your hand,
binding together all other fallible people.

Like the binding of a wound.

❧   ❧

CREDIT WHERE CREDIT'S DUE

The epigram on pg. 4 appears in *Donald Judd's Writings*, ed. by Flavin Judd and Caitlin Murray, published by The Judd Foundation/David Zwirner, 2017. I encountered it in a review of that collection entitled "A Visionary of the Real," written by Jed Perl that appeared in *The New York Review of Books,* 54:16, pgs. 30-33.

In "Passions and Pigeons," pgs. 10 and 11, the reference to Samuel Beckett's Belacqua in *More Pricks than Kicks* appears in the "A Wet Night" section, pg. 50 in the 1977 Picador Edition.

In "Whistling While You Work," pg. 20, the Eric Hoffer observation can be found in his 1971 book, *First Things, Last Things,* published by Hopewell, pg. 43.

In "Dream Work," pg. 22, the epigram is from Eric Hoffer's *Truth Imagined,* published by Hopewell in 1983, pg. 3.

In "Shifting Gears: Tools of the Trade," pgs. 26 and 27, the epigram is from Philip Larkin's poem that appears on page 106 of his *Collected Poems*, Ed. by Anthony Thwaite, The Noonday Press, Farrar, Straus, Giroux, 1988. The reference to Thomas Hardy's poems includes words drawn from "The Darkling Thrush," "The Contretemps," and a few other Hardy poems. The shifting meaning of *shiftless* can be confirmed by comparing an earlier and a newer edition of *The Oxford English Dictionary.*

In "Heaven at the Club One-Eleven," pg. 28, the epigram is taken from Richard Hugo's "The Hilltop."

The full poem can be found in *The Collected Poems of Richard Hugo,* NY: Norton, 1984, reissued with Intro by William Kittredge, NY: Norton, 2007, pg. 249. The Beckett quote is from one of Belacqua's musings in the "Dante and the Lobster" chapter in Samuel Beckett's *More Pricks than Kicks.*

In "Love," pg. 42, the beginning quotation is from Franz Schubert's manuscript "My Dream." Music critics suggest Schubert was thinking of his song cycle *Die Wintereise* in this passage.

The Epigram on pg. 50 paraphrases a conversation held between banjo players extraordinaire Béla Fleck, Abigail Washburn, and host Krista Tippett that aired on PBS's "On Being," November 24, 2016.

In "Closure," pg. 57, the Tess Gallagher poem "Small Garden Near a Field," written after the death of her brother, can be found in *Amplitude: New and Selected Poems*, St. Paul, MN: Graywolf Press, pg. 171.

In "It Goes Without Saying," pg. 67, the quote is included in Linda Greenhouse's "How Smart Women Got the Chance," a review appearing in *The New York Review of Books,* April 6, 2017, of Nancy Weiss Malkiel's *'Keep the Damned Women Out': The Struggle for Coeducation.* Princeton University Press, 2017. Both Malkiel and Greenhouse's writings reconfirm the value of Susanne Langer's observations in *Philosophy in a New Key*, as pertinent today as when that book was published in 1941.

"For Don Belton," pgs. 68-69, pays homage to him, and to our friendship. He was the author of the novel *Around Midnight* appearing in 1986, editor of the anthology *Speak My Name: Black Men on Masculinity and the American Dream* in 1996, and writer of short stories appearing in numerous publications.

In the Intro to Part VI, pg. 74, the line from "The Importance of Elsewhere" can be found in Philip Larkin's *Collected Poems*, ed. by Anthony Thwaite, The Noonday Press, Farrar, Straus, Giroux, 1988, pg. 104.

In "Veganomics," pgs. 76-77, the epigram is taken from the "Whale as a Dish" chapter of *Moby Dick.*

In "Language Acquisition II," pg. 78, the first references are to a collection of wonderful newspaper pieces by Hattie Blossom Fritze reprinted in *Horse and Buggy Days on Old Cape Cod: Reminiscences of the Town of Barnstable by an 83 year old Native.* Great Marshes Press, 1966. pgs. 33 and 71.

  The words mentioned, including *tombolo*, can be found in Eugene Green and William L. Sachse, *Names of the Land: Cape Cod, Nantucket, Martha's Vineyard and the Elizabeth Islands.* Chester, CN.: Globe Pequot Press, ca 1983.

  The explanation for the word *tortience* can be found in Elizabeth Reynard's *The Narrow Land: Folk Chronicles of Old Cape Cod*, first published in 1934, reprinted numerous times by the Chatham Historical Society, most recently in 1993. The wonderful description of Mary Walley, the minister's daughter, can be found on page 126 of the 1993 reprint.

In "Midden in the Front Yard," pgs. 84-85, the information was gleaned from sources too numerous to mention here. They include Delores Bird Carpenter's *Early Encounters: Native Americans and Europeans in New England: from the Papers of W. Sears Nickerson,* published by Michigan State University Press in 1994; Frederick Freeman's *Civilization and Barbarism,*

Illustrated by especial reference to Metacomet and the Extinction of His Race. Cambridge Riverside Press, 1878; *Indian History of Harwich, Massachusetts,* published by The Harwich Historical Society in 1972; Josiah Paine's *A History of Harwich, Barnstable County, Massachusetts 1620-1800,* published in 1937, reprinted by Parnassus Imprints in 1971; and also from a series of five small books/pamphlets entitled *Biographies and Legends of the New England Indians,* published by Leo Bonfanti as part of the New England Historical Series and Pride Publications in 1968; *Mourt's Relation: A Journal of the English Plantation Settled at Plymouth,* anonymously printed in 1622 and possibly written by Edward Winslow and William Bradford, or by George Morton. It is available in numerable formats published by numerous presses.

In "Late Life Blooming," pp. 96-97, the epigram is from Miles Davis' autobiography, *Miles: The Autobiography,* written in collaboration with Quincy Troupe. New York: Simon and Schuster, 1989, pg. 74.

In "The Swimmer," pgs. 98-99, the Kafka passage in its entirety is: "Man is a free and secure citizen of the world, for he is fettered to a chain...long enough to give him the freedom of all earthly space, and yet only so long that nothing can drag him past the frontiers of the world. But simultaneously he is a free and secure citizen of Heaven as well, for he is also fettered by a similarly designed heavenly chain. So that if he heads, say, for the earth, his heavenly collar throttles him, and if he heads for Heaven, the earthly one does the same. And yet all the possibilities are his, and he feels it, more, he actually refuses to account for the deadlock by an error in the original fettering."
This passage can be found in the "Paradise" section of a collection gathered from Kafka's diaries, letters, notebooks and fiction, edited and published in 1958 by

Nahum N. Glatzer in *Parables and Paradoxes*, or in the Third Notebook, an entry of November 24, 1917: "Both the man in ecstasy and the man drowning throw up their hands." Collected in *The Blue Octavo Notebooks*, ed. Max Brod, tr. Ernst Kaiser and Eithne Williams. Cambridge, MA. by Exact Change, 1991.

In "No Footprints," pg. 100, the epigram consists of lines taken from the late Stanley Kunitz' poem entitled "Passing Through—On My seventy-ninth Birthday."

In "Weeding, pg. 103, the epigram that appears can be found among Franz Schubert's writings in his notebooks.

In "The Things we Carry: Ancestors Packing," pgs. 108-109, the epigram is from Robert Sapolsky's *Behave: The Biology of Humans at Our Best and Worst,* NY: Penguin Press, 2017. The brief bios in this poem refer to the lives of my eight great-grandparents. Their full stories can be found in my *From Green Fields to Blue Collars: Resistance and Persistence in Four Ohio and Michigan Families, 1870-1930,* published in 2015.

In "Yup'ik Tears," pg. 110, the epigram is from Pablo Neruda's "El Pueblo in Plenos Poderes," sometimes published as just "El Pueblo." It can be found among other places in *Neruda: Selected Poems,* edited by Nathaniel Tarn.

My description of the work of Native Alaskan women in the Northernmost parts of Canada in early times was inspired by a passage of extraordinary detail in *Famous Book of the Eskimos*, collected and edited by Dagmar Freuchen, published by Fawcett Premier in 1961. Peter Freuchen first visited the area in 1906, continuing to visit, eventually living and working there for two decades, married for ten years to "a beautiful

Eskimo girl named Navarana." From his precise and very graphic description of the Caribou Eskimos: "Their women were robust... their life and work...so difficult as to mark them completely....In winter...[they] had to...scrape aside the snow to get to the heather, and since they...had to save their mittens, they pulled the heather loose with bare hands...at a temperature of forty below. Their hands were completely malformed, black, hard to the feel as if made of wood....They let their nails grow very long... the general impression was that of sinister bird claws. When they came home in winter with their fuel, they couldn't burn it under the open sky, for that would use it up too quickly. Cooking wasn't possible in the snow house either, as the snow would melt....They would build a small, low hut, with a hole in the roof....in there the woman would lie down to do the cooking. She had to blow on the fire continually to keep it going, ashes would fly around her face, hair, and shoulders, and her eyes were always red and watering, so that the tears made deep grooves of bare skin down over... [her] dirt-covered face." (pgs. 15-16)

In "Last Confession," pgs. 112-113, the epigram comes from a letter Franz Kafka wrote to Oskar Pollak, January 27, 1904. It can be found in *Letters to Friends, Family, and Editors.* Trans. Richard and Clara Winston. NY: Schocken Books, 1977.

On the back cover blurb, "No Ideas But in Things" is of course taken from poet William Carlos Williams' *Paterson,* which appeared in five volumes between 1946 and 1958.

Finally, credit is due to my dear friend of almost seventy years Jenni Walz Loynd, who in her usual generous and self-effacing way suggested, and even demonstrated, how her image could be cut from the back cover photo here so as not to confuse readers about whose hand had written these pages. Writer, friend, wife, mother, grandmother, hostess and healer extraordinaire, she has chronicled in detail and with many photographs her family's history in *The Black Swamp Find: A True Story about the Life of Carl and Jennie Hench and Their Grandchildren's Surprise Discovery*, as well as written a biography of her dearly-missed sister Toni. Thank you, Jenni, for your support, and thank you, Dr. Robert Loynd, for snapping the photo of the two of us on a recent happy October day on the same beach this solitary walker still walks every day.

www.ingramcontent.com/pod-product-compliance
Lightning Source LLC
Chambersburg PA
CBHW061745020426
42331CB00006B/1359